HOW TO BELONG When You're Already a Member

John G. Kerbs

PACIFIC PRESS PUBLISHING ASSOCIATION
Mountain View, California
Oshawa, Ontario

First printing published in 1981.

Library of Congress Cataloging in Publication Data

Kerbs, John G.
How to belong when you're already a member.

1. Assurance (Theology) I. Title
BT785.K44 248.4'8673 81-38346
ISBN 0-8163-0437-8 AACR2

Design by Ichiro Nakashima

To my wife, Nancy, and my three sons, Jeff, Jim, and John, who by just being themselves have helped me to learn much of what I know about God's love.

Preface

An earnest young man asked me some time ago, "What *do you* believe?" He seemed somewhat bewildered by various discussions regarding the basic elements of salvation. Is not our hope in what Christ alone has done for us on the cross? Why then give emphasis to the possibility and importance of overcoming sin?

A young woman expressed confusion after a speaker at a Bible conference said, "Sanctification has nothing to do with our salvation." Some understood what he was attempting to say, but can such statements be misleading?

In a series of five informal early-morning talks at a camp meeting, I attempted to set forth those beliefs, attitudes, and commitments which have to do with a saving relationship with God. These talks have resulted in this little book. Much of the conversational style remains. Theological terms have been for the most part deliberately avoided.

Back to the question put to me, "What do you believe?" Though certainly imperfectly expressed, this is my answer to this young friend and to any others who like him may be trying to put together the basics of salvation. It is my testimony to those who are seeking for not only assurance now, but also understanding of how to maintain a saving relationship with God.

The title, *How to Belong When You're Already a Member*, was prompted by this statement made by Ellen

White. "Almost but not wholly saved means to be not almost but wholly lost."—*Selected Messages*, bk. 1, p. 400. How is this possible if the "way of salvation" is "so plain that a little child can walk in it"?—*Messages to Young People*, p. 15. What is involved in *walking in* the way of salvation?

If we are assured of our acceptance with God, certain of salvation if life should suddenly end, how shall we then live? How can we relate properly to trials and temptation? What do the "three angels' messages" and church membership have to do with it all?

May the Holy Spirit enlighten our minds as we consider these questions together.

John G. Kerbs

Contents

God Loves You—Do You Believe It?

I awakened in an ambulance as it screamed down a desert road in southern California. Choking on my own blood and dimly conscious of a torn, broken body, I was certain my end had come. Slowly it all came back. A car had come lurching out of control into our lane at high speed. And now I was concerned about only two things—those I would leave behind and my own preparation for eternity. I committed my bride of a few months to the care of God and in uncomplicated faith accepted, without pleading, forgiveness of my sins, so freely available at the hand of my high priest, Jesus, in the heavenly sanctuary. I lapsed again into unconsciousness, with the peace of complete assurance that life everlasting was mine in Jesus.

At Thanksgiving time in my boyhood church in Sacramento, Pastor Raymond Libby gave the Sabbath morning pulpit to the congregation to share their blessings with one another. Each person was invited to come forward and share a blessing for which he was very grateful. At one of these Thanksgiving services, I recall hearing expressions of gratitude for health and wealth, success and protection, family and love, and other gifts. Then the line to the pulpit shortened and ended. Pastor Libby stood back waiting for more to come. Finally he stepped to the pulpit and asked, "Isn't there anyone here who is thankful his sins are forgiven?" He added with feeling, "I'm thankful that God has forgiven my sins!"

So often we are most thankful for the things we don't need; and for that which we need the very most, we fail to thank God, either taking it for granted or not being certain we possess it. However old or young you may be, there is only one thing you really need, only one thing—and you need it even more than life itself. To be alive in this world is not really your great need; life here is a gift that comes and goes like all earthly blessings. None are unaware that life can end suddenly and unexpectedly. Life here has within it no promise of endlessness. There is only one thing we really need, and that is to be assured our sins are forgiven. Do you really have that assurance today? Perhaps you look at older Christians and think their assurance of acceptance with God is rather automatic, based on the assumption that sinning is for them a thing of the past.

Some people young and old, go through a time when they really doubt their own religious experience—because they are very conscious of sin in their lives. In order to escape the problem of sin, they pretend not to be near God. (One young person told me if he mistreated God long enough, He would leave him alone. God never does, of course; He keeps reaching out after us.) Being somewhat aware of both God's holiness and His love, we are thrown into conflict. We are told that "the strongest temptation cannot excuse sin."—*Messages to Young People*, p. 62. And that troubles us. We are admonished not to make of sin a light matter. We are reminded that God hates sin so badly it simply cannot dwell in His presence. And yet we are urged not to be anxious or troubled about our sins! "We are not to be anxious about what Christ and God think about us, but about what God thinks of Christ, our Substitute." *Selected Messages*, bk. 2, pp. 32, 33.

How do we get rid of this anxiety about sin? We can't forget Hebrews 9:27 which assures us, "It is appointed unto men once to die, but after this the judgment." No second chance. That terrifies us and makes us afraid of death at times. Scripture reminds us we're sinners. "If we say we have no sin, we deceive ourselves, and the truth is not in us." "If we say that we have not sinned, we make him a liar." 1 John 1:8, 10. "All we like sheep have gone astray; we have turned every one to his own way." Isaiah 53:6. Of course, God, in reminding us of our sinfulness, was hoping to frighten us of ourselves and of the devil; instead, we sometimes become afraid of Him. It was never God's intention that we fear Him in this sense. He wanted us to be so distrustful of ourselves and so wary of the devil that we would flee *to* Him, not away from Him. He has made this very clear. Yet sometimes just the opposite happens. We conclude that God really is not big enough and loving enough to provide a remedy for sinners such as we are. He can care for the sins of others, we think, because they are not of so great variety and so often repeated as ours. They seem to face sin, overcome it, and move on. But as for us, we do the same thing over and over again. At times the very problem over which we thought we had gained a victory crops up again. Does this describe your experience?

To make us further hesitant to approach God, the very attitude of some toward the sins of their fellow human beings causes us to create a God in their image. Have you ever said, "I'm sorry," and received the reply, "You said that last time"? or "I'm sorry too"? People often decline our apologies and fail to respond to our pleas for forgiveness. Almost inevitably we begin to think God is like that. He may be misrepresented by someone telling a youth, "We'll give you one more chance." So we believe God will give us *one* more chance. And in our self-confidence we promise we'll never bother Him again with a particular sin. We think we have really made it; we have finally overcome and thank Him for it. And then we find ourselves falling again into sins quite similar to those we thought were conquered. We are tempted to despair. We conclude that like these human beings we have disappointed so often, God also has a limit to his forgiveness.

We can learn something about God's kind of forgiveness from a little child. Is there something more beautiful and Christlike about a little child than those who are older? Do we by nature grow less and less like God? One godlike characteristic of a little child is that a child can forgive very readily. I foolishly punished one of my young sons for a misdeed in which he had had no part. When I discovered my error, I wondered if he would forgive me for being so unfair. I mentioned his memory verse for the week, "Forgive, and ye shall be forgiven" (Luke 6:37), hoping he would forgive his hasty dad. But this softening up was unnecessary. When I asked, "Please forgive me," he replied, with tears still on his cheeks, "I already have." I'll never forget those beautiful words and have often thought, *God is like that.*

If we are unforgiving, we not only misrepresent God, but we give evidence that we ourselves have not yet received the pardoning love of God. See *Christ's Object Lessons*, p. 251. The attitude of forgiveness toward others comes with accepting forgiveness from God. Our ability to forgive is a good index of whether we really believe God has accepted and forgiven us. A woman once told me about the sins her sister in the church had committed against her. Detecting bitterness, I asked, "And have you forgiven her?" With narrowed eyes she said, "I will never forgive her until she confesses. The Bible says you've got to confess before you are forgiven!"

While it is certainly true that we are to confess our sins, this is not to take the form of an effort to persuade God, or His true children, to forgive us. When we confess our sins, it is only to receive the forgiveness *already there*. The soldiers kneeling beside Jesus, not confessing their sins but driving cruel nails into His hands and feet, may have heard Him say, "Father, forgive them; for they know not what they do." Luke 23:34. You can be assured if any Roman soldier came to Christ at a later date saying "Forgive me," He could reply, "I already have." We must understand it that way. Forgiveness withheld, by man or God, until confession is made cannot be forgiveness at all. God has not held a grudge against us, ready to destroy us until we come crawling to Him in penitence. He has given us His love freely, completely, immediately. "While we were yet sinners, Christ died for us." Romans 5:8. The Lamb of God was "slain from the foundation of the world." Revelation 13:8. Long ago He triumphed over sin—our sin. If we don't believe God is big enough and loving enough to care for *our* sins, we begin to make of sin something other than sin. It becomes hereditary weakness or just sinful tendency or just "being human"—infirmity of the flesh. We hesitate to keep bothering God with our sins.

I am *not* suggesting that we can never experience victory. I am saying that victory does not always come as we wish it would—instantly, completely, the moment we recognize that sin is sin. We can hate sin and still sin; "we may make mistakes, but we will hate the sin that caused the sufferings of the Son of God." *Selected Messages*, bk. 1, p. 360. This is not to encourage us to continue sinning while we profess to hate sin but to urge that we not doubt God's love and forgiveness when we find ourselves sometimes doing the very things we really don't want to do. Keep coming to Him, thousands of times and more. Keep calling sin by its right name—sin. As long as we keep believing God loves sinners and has invited us to come to him as we are, with all our struggles with sin—as long as we keep coming to Him, we will be in "no wise cast out." John 6:37.

We sometimes sing the hymn that contains the words "Father, we come to Thee, turn not away," with a note of anxiety, as though He may turn away. Even the men of Scripture seemed at times fearful that God would turn away from them as they confessed their forsaken sins. The repentant sinner need never fear that God, the ruler of a trillion galaxies, is so small He is going to turn away from one of His children because of some little sin. Little sin? There are no little sins, you say. And you're correct, but in the light of God's bigness, His greatness, and the capacity He has for love and forgiveness, based on His more-than-abundant atonement for sin with all its related problems, sin, however grave, is overcome by grace. It is not for him a hard matter to care for. He has already poured out all Heaven to do just that. All the resources have been provided, and we must not be worried that God is turning away just because of something we have done.

A woman, elderly now, had been in the church for many years. The pastor noticed her constant anxiety about wanting to do more and more good things—more missionary work, more Bible studies, more literature, more territory. All were legitimate and necessary Christian activities. But one day, with concerned perception, he asked, "Sister, don't you ever have any peace?" She wept. Years ago she had committed a terrible sin, and all these years she had been trying to make up for it by doing missionary work.

What a tragedy when we think God is not big enough to take whatever sin, however oft repeated and repented of, and cast it into "the depths of the sea." Micah 7:19.

Have you noticed what immediately follows those passages in Scripture which remind us we are sinners? "The wages of sin is death; but the gift of God is eternal life." Romans 6:23. "All we like sheep have gone astray; we have turned every one to his own way." But don't stop there. What next? The Lord hath laid on him the iniquity of us all." Isaiah 53:6. "If we say that we have no sin, we deceive ourselves." 1 John 1:8. And the next verse, "If we confess our sins, he is faithful and just to forgive us our sins, and to cleanse us from all unrighteousness." And verse 10, "If we say we have not sinned, we make him a liar." But what is the assurance given right after that? "My little children, these things write I unto you, that ye sin not. And if any man sin, we have an advocate with the Father, Jesus Christ the righteous."

In the original Scriptures there were no commas, no verse divisions, no chapter divisions to divide promise from threat. These were all added much later for our convenience, but at times to our confusion. In God's mind it all went together; and we must never, never forget that when He reminds us of our sins, it is not to frighten us of Him but to bring us to Him. He is the only one who can handle the problem of sin, and anything we may do without Him is wasted effort.

We cannot earn God's love and forgiveness. In the front of some Bibles "indulgences" are often offered for reading Scripture fifteen minutes daily. When you spend your hour with God, is He keeping track of the time, measuring the soreness of your knees and the length of your prayers, or counting the chapters you read? We need to be on our knees. We need to read the Book. But don't let Satan cause you to think God is especially pleased or appeased by the amount of time we are spending reading His Book or praying to Him.

He does not measure even our faith; faith is not meritorious. It earns nothing. Faith is only an instrument by which we can lay hold upon the righteousness of God. There is absolutely nothing we can do, or must do, to earn His favor.

I was once scheduled to speak at a state prison and was frightened. What was I going to say to these "hardened criminals"?

On a previous visit I had been told of death row, where all waited either to be "hanged by the neck until dead" or to be killed by a seven-gun firing squad. The prisoners told us if they went to a certain window, they could actually see it happen—a hood over the head, a wall behind, the sound of the rifles, and instant death.

With this picture in mind I faced these prisoners who were expecting a message of hope. I asked the little group, "When a man gets on death row, is there any way he can ever get off?"

The first reply: "No way. Once they are on death row they just wait till the date when they die." Another said, with only the faintest trace of hope, "Sometimes they put the wrong man on death row—they make a mistake. When they find the right man, they release the other one."

"At this point I reminded them of the sinner's plight: "The wages of sin is death." Romans 6:23. "The soul that sinneth, it shall die." Ezekiel 18:4. "Now perhaps," I continued, "someone can find out that I'm not a sinner, you're not a sinner. Though the wages of sin is death, they've got the wrong man!" Each one knew even without reading Scripture that he *was* the one. And there in that church service behind bars, every one of us was placed on death row, whether inside that prison or outside. All we like sheep had gone astray. Everyone had turned to his own way. Isaiah 53:6. Everyone had sinned; none were righteous, no, not one. Romans 3:9, 10. All humanity is on death row, and not a being in this universe, not God Himself, can ever conclude the wrong one has been accused or that any can be released on the basis of a mistake.

I pressed the question further, "Isn't there some other way a man on death row can finally be released and go free?" They thought hard, but none could think of any. I continued, "If the only way you can get off death row is to be proved innocent, then we're all in a very bad spot, aren't we?" They agreed. I then asked, "Have you ever heard of a man who is really guilty, knows he's guilty, admits he's guilty, but still is granted a pardon by a governor, a king, a queen, a president, or some military officer? Have you ever heard of a pardon like that?"

By this analogy I was able to share with them the same promises we have shared in this chapter, promising we can be pardoned because "the Lord hath laid on Him the iniquity of us all." Isaiah 53:6. We need not concern ourselves with our guilt. All our guiltiness must be laid at the foot of the cross.

A message addressed by Ellen White to a troubled soul

long ago urges that "the feeling of guiltiness must be laid at the foot of the cross."—*Testimonies to Ministers*, p. 518. Not because you are not guilty. You are guilty, and "the sense of sin has poisoned the springs of life. But Christ says, 'I will take your sins; I will give you peace.' "—*The Ministry of Healing*, p.85. "Banish no longer your self-respect"—*Testimonies to Ministers*, p. 520. Isn't it beautiful that God is actually concerned about our self-respect, that He doesn't want us to be casting ourselves down and down, always looking down upon ourselves? Again He says, Destroy "no longer your self-respect; for I have bought you with the price of My own blood. You are Mine. Your weakened will I will strengthen. Your remorse for sin I will remove."—*Testimonies to Ministers*, p. 520. You notice that He wants to remove your *remorse* for sin. Does that seem strange? Should not the remorse remain though the sin is gone? No. There is a time when the remorse is also removed. A time when we must quit smiting ourselves. Webster defines *remorse* as "a gnawing distress arising from a sense of guilt for past wrongs." God says, "your remorse for sin I will remove." "Then turn your grateful heart, trembling with uncertainty, and lay hold upon the hope set before you. God accepts your broken, contrite heart. He offers you free pardon. He offers to adopt you into His family, with His grace to help your weakness, and the dear Jesus will lead you on step by step if you will only put your hand in his and let Him guide you."—*Mind, Character, and Personality*, vol. 2, p. 451. How beautiful! How wonderful! Praise Him for such love!

"As far as the east is from the west, so far hath he removed our transgressions from us." Psalm 103:12. How far is east from west? Can you measure it? Travel 25,000 miles around the earth and you still haven't measured the distance between east and west. Yet God had chosen that meaningful expression before most men knew the world was round. And you've all seen the morning fog, thicker than darkness—and suddenly it's gone. You didn't even notice it go. That's the way He has swept away your sins! He has "swept away your transgressions like a cloud, and your sins like mist." Isaiah 44:22, RSV. He casts our sins into the depths of the sea. Micah 7:19. He has promised to cast all our sins behind His back. Isaiah 38:17. God knew it would be a difficult task to convince us He will fully pardon. There is good reason why He has—over and over and over again, throughout Scripture and other inspired messages—reminded us to stop worrying about our past sins.

The devil very subtly and successfully causes us to dwell upon the sins of yesterday. One of his crafty and most successful designs is to tempt us to dwell upon our past sins, even with abhorrence. And what happens? It is well expressed in Alexander Pope's "Essay on Man." "Vice is a monster of so frightful mien, / As to be hated needs but to be seen: / Yet seen too oft, familiar with her face, / We first endure, then pity, then embrace." We often apply this idea to young people and tell them to avoid bad movies, television shows, and reading, for if the activities are continued long enough they won't look bad anymore. And that's true. But Satan has other ways to cause us to dwell upon sin. Those of us who would never think of looking at a bad television program, going to a movie, or reading a novel will be tempted to read our own minds, our own memories and to dwell upon the past sin in our lives. There are always people who say, "If you only knew my past—" But everyone has some gray pages, at least in thought, plan, motive, and imagination, which he would rather no one read, not even God. Everyone has something in his past which Satan can tempt him to dwell upon with abhorrence.

How Satan must rejoice when we begin smiting ourselves. The process often has begun this way. "Was that really *me*? Did *I* do that? How could *I* have done it? Were those *my* thoughts?" Satan delights in repeatedly bringing your life record up in the mind until you loathe yourself.

Then comes the demand for self-protection, a need at times just to preserve your own sanity. So you begin to make excuses. You begin to think it wasn't really your fault after all. Somebody else made you do it. "If it hadn't been for him, I wouldn't have done it. It's my heredity, my weakness." Thus we begin to "endure," to "pity" and to become a little more comfortable with our loathsome past, sheerly for self-protection.

And what did Pope say? "We first endure, then pity, then *embrace*." Perhaps all of us have experienced this. We have found ourselves right back into the very thing we thought we hated so badly, "embracing" the very thing we thought we loathed and were trying to escape. All our efforts to get away from it failed. The reason? We put it in the wrong place—self. We didn't cast it upon the Lord and allow him to remove it. We failed to stop smiting ourselves for it over and over again. For a lifetime some people keep harboring and dwelling upon some terrible memories of their past lives while these memories accumulate still others. They may be driven either to total despair or to encapsulating their past into something they no longer call sin. And so they excuse those sins and consequently others which they continue to commit.

As long as we allow a barrier of this sort to continue between us and God, as long as we do not believe that He accepts us and genuinely forgives all our sins, we cannot experience victory. "If the enemy can lead the desponding to take their eyes off from Jesus, and look to themselves, and dwell upon their own unworthiness, instead of dwelling upon the worthiness of Jesus, His love, His merits, His great mercy, he will get away their shield of faith and gain his object; they will be exposed to his fiery temptation."—*Early Writings*, p. 73. Deliverance from sin comes in one marvelous package. When we accept that God has really accepted us, when we know He has forgiven us and that He takes the repentant sinner just as he is without placing him on probation, then we are on the road to victory. Until that time we don't have a shield, and we are exposed to his fiery temptations. How? By looking to ourselves, dwelling upon our own unworthiness "instead of dwelling upon the worthiness of Jesus, His love, His merits, His great mercy."

Jesus "did not refuse the simplest flower plucked by the hand of a child, and offered to him in love. He accepted the offerings of children, and blessed the givers." And what else did He do? He inscribed "their names in the book of life."—*The Desire of Ages*, p. 564. Astounding! A little child brought Jesus a simple flower he had plucked. And Jesus put his name in the book of life! Remember—being in or out of the book of life is what it's all about. It will ultimately decide one's eternal destiny!

Revelation reminds us a number of times that those who are saved are the ones whose names are written in the book and that those who are cast into the lake of fire are the ones whose names are not written there. When the disciples came rejoicing over the fact that the devils were subject to their command and that the sick were healed, Jesus cautioned, Don't rejoice in this, but rejoice that your names are written above. Now here is a little child bringing in love to Jesus a flower, maybe a dandelion wilted in a chubby hand—nothing that in itself could earn favor, not an orchid corsage—just a little wild flower plucked on the hillside. And to think this little love gift is accepted and that the little one's name *is inscribed in the book of life!*

Think of the implications of this disarmingly simple incident. If a child can get his name in that easily, why can't you do the same? You may reply, If He can enter it so quickly and easily, can't He erase it just as quickly and easily? But it seems unlikely that God is going to quickly blot out your name when you make a mistake. What about those children on the hillsides of Galilee whose names He placed in the book of life? As they became teenagers and thought some "bad things" and made mistakes, did He blot theirs out?

Are young people tempted to believe that? They may have felt rather comfortable about their religious experience in the fourth, fifth, and sixth grades, but now with new desires welling up in their hearts, they find themselves thinking some new thoughts. They may at times feel passionate, rebellious, or unsettled. Are their names then blotted out? Surely not. The only way you will ever get your name blotted out of the book of life is by looking away from Jesus so long He can no longer get your attention, till you reach the point when He knows you will never turn back to Him again.

Of course, it's dangerous to wander. You may get lost. But it's absolutely fatal to believe you're shut out of the Father's house each time you stray from the path, even though you want to return. If you are the greatest theologian in the church, there's only one way for you to be saved. Only one for anyone. Whether you are illiterate or have three graduate degrees, it matters not—there is only one way to be accepted of the Lord. And that is to simply look to Him in faith; to, figuratively, pluck a little flower and offer it to Him in love, believing He loves you and accepting that love. He has promised to forgive your sins, to cast them into the depths of the sea and to accept you as you are with your multitude of imperfections.

God loves you with an everlasting love, with a tenacious love that will not easily let you go. He wants to save you so badly that there is nothing you could do to change His desire to live with you eternally. You may make Him weep, but He never weeps for Himself. He weeps only because of His love for you.

He wants so much to save us, but often He can't get and hold our attention long enough. That's God's biggest problem. He has the power to save, to abundantly pardon, but He is frequently unable to hold our gaze upon His love completely enough and consistently enough to save us. We look away and become afraid; we forget and doubt our way into despair and oblivion. This need not be.

Our Father, how great You are; how loving You are. Yet how little we think about and understand this love. Forgive us for dwelling upon ourselves. Forgive us for doubting Your goodness. We know You rejoice in the fact that we come to You as we are—sinful, helpless, weak. We cast ourselves anew upon Your mercy and ask You to blot out all our transgressions. Give us that rejoicing heart which only You can give, as we know we are accepted by You, the God of the universe, who is love. We pray in Jesus' name. Amen.

Almost Saved—What Makes the Difference?

We were returning to Johannesburg from a camp meeting in Cape Town, South Africa. One of my young sons had learned a new song. He sang as we drove, "I've got the joy, joy, joy, joy down in my heart." He got through that stanza pretty well. But when he came to the stanza about the devil—"I know the devil doesn't like it, but it's down in my heart"—he got a little mixed up. He sang lustily, "I know the devil doesn't like me, but he's down in my heart!" Many of us could sing that couldn't we? We have few doubts about what the devil intends for us. We know he doesn't like us. We know rather well he wants to destroy us. And yet we all too often allow him down in our hearts.

God values very highly the free will of man. For a reason we cannot fully grasp, God allows us to have what we choose. He even allows us to be lost if we do not desire otherwise. At times we may feel as my seven-year-old son felt when he asked, "Why doesn't God just *make* me be good?" Have you ever felt that way? He knows what we need. Why doesn't He just save us? Why do I have to do anything? Doesn't God do everything toward my salvation anyway? Yes, in a sense He does, but there is one thing I must do. I must respond to, give in to, accept, surrender to His love. Here is where many of us fail. Not because we don't surrender *something*, but because we don't surrender *everything*.

In chapter 1 we presented a God who really loves *you*, and we must never doubt that. He really wants to save you regardless of who you are or what you are or what you have or haven't done. He loves with an eager, tenacious love, reaching out after you and me. His problem is getting our attention and getting us to respond. The song says, "The Saviour is waiting to enter your heart. . . . Oh, how He wants to come in." But the question which presents the problem is "Why don't you *let* Him come in?"

In this chapter we will speak of the tragedy of half-surrender. The saddest chapters in the Bible, in history and in your life and mine are those of people who attempt to give God *something* of their lives—but not *everything*.

Remember the little children in chapter 1 who came to Jesus with flowers? You can be assured when Jesus wrote those names in the book of life, He saw a complete, trusting response. It is not with a half-heart that a little child comes to Jesus. He sees in Jesus a loving Saviour and responds with everything he has. All that the children in our story had were roadside flowers, but that's what they gave, and it was enough—it was everything.

In the book *Messages to Young People*, page 30, Ellen White reminds, "The surrender of all our powers to God greatly simplifies the problem of life." And, she continues, this total, complete surrender "cuts short a thousand struggles with the passions of the natural heart."

These struggles always come over the matter of surrender, the matter of *giving* some of our powers, but not all, to the Father who is ever pleading, "Give me thine heart." Proverbs 23:26.

To the little child the look of Jesus means only love. He doesn't see all that we see. When we get a little older, the look of Jesus reveals also our sinfulness. One look at the Saviour makes painfully distinct the evil in our lives. At the same time, we must look long enough, while still aware of our sinfulness and unworthiness, to see also His look of love and forgiveness.

Peter saw that. Peter looked long enough. You will remember he had repeatedly denied his Lord, even finally with cursing and swearing. What terrible things he must have said in his effort to totally disassociate himself from the Saviour; perhaps derogatory statements about the One whom he really loved. But it was done, and it was bad. When his eyes met those of Jesus there in the judgment hall, his true condition came to him with tremendous force. He went out and wept bitterly, but something about that look said more than "You're a traitor, Peter." He saw in that look of Jesus complete love, complete compassion, complete forgiveness.

And that was the difference between Peter and Judas. Judas could have done the same thing. It was never Jesus' will that Judas go out and hang himself. Sometimes we read the story of Judas as though his tragic end was inevitable. No. Had Judas only looked to Jesus with genuine repentance as Peter did, even after receiving the thirty pieces of silver, even though too late to return them and buy back the Saviour. Had he looked to Jesus, had he been concerned about his sin rather than the results of it, he could have seen the Saviour's look of pity. True, Judas had gone too far to turn back, but it was not the Saviour who shut him out. Overwhelmed by his own guilt, he placed himself forever beyond the reach of Christ's saving love.

What was Judas's problem? Most of you have discovered long ago that Judas was really a "good man." By outward standards, of then and now, he would have been considered a man of considerable integrity—one of the finest. All, including Judas, agreed that he was the best disciple of the group, that to lose him would be the greatest of losses.

Yet we seldom put ourselves in the category of Judas. Peter or Thomas, perhaps, but not Judas. We've written him off as determinedly wicked and rarely identify with him. Let's listen to an enlightening description of Judas.

"He felt in his own person the evidence of Christ's power." Now that's Judas we're talking about. "He recognized the teaching of Christ as superior to all that he had ever heard. He loved the Great Teacher." He really loved the Great Teacher and desired to be with Him. Not only that, he desired to be like Him. "He felt a desire to be changed in character and life, and he hoped to experience this through connecting himself with Jesus."—*The Desire of Ages*, p. 717. He recognized Him as the greatest of men. He loved Him. He felt power in his life in connecting with Him. And he hoped to experience a change in his character and life. Judas's motive in joining the disciples was not to get into the money bag. Furthermore, he was an evangelist; he healed the sick and cast out devils. That's Judas. See *The Desire of Ages*, p. 717.

Now there were some things wrong with Judas. Judas did not come to the point of surrendering himself fully to Christ. He did not give up his worldly ambition or his love of money. He cultivated a disposition to criticize and accuse. Judas "determined not to unite himself so closely to Christ but that he could draw away."—*The Desire of Ages*, p. 719. And that's where Judas failed. He would not surrender *everything*—his worldly ambitions, his love of money, his high opinion of his own qualifications. He looked upon his brethren as greatly inferior to himself in judgment and ability. Much of the dissension among the disciples about position in the coming kingdom was instigated and inspired by Judas. All of these are also modern, respectable sins, but nonetheless very dangerous, very deadly. The saddest stories of all Scripture are of those who followed God, but with reservations.

Look at Amaziah in 2 Chronicles 25. In the books called Kings and Chronicles we find the stories of the kings of Judah and Israel. Many chapters, as does this one, begin with the king's name, his age, the name of one or both his parents, and the kingdom over which he reigned, Israel or Judah. And then it is often declared whether he did what was right or whether he did what was evil in the sight of the Lord. The greatest number of them, practically every king in Israel and most in Judah, did evil. A few were declared good, but some, and Amaziah is one, tried to be both.

Of Amaziah it is said (in verse 2), "He did that which was right in the sight of the Lord, but not with a perfect heart." Amaziah's service was not with the whole or entire heart. Moffatt says he served God, "but not with an undivided mind." The subtlety, the danger, the tragedy of this type of service is that a person who serves God, but not with his whole heart, usually looks rather good. Even the person himself may be unaware of or have rationalized his true condition. That's why we must be sensitive and responsive to every appeal the Spirit of Christ makes to our hearts.

Let's read about Amaziah's life (in verse 4). "He slew not their children." When he came to the throne, he executed the assasins of his father, who had been king before him. This was legal and even necessary. "But he slew not their children, but did as it is written in the law in the book of Moses, where the Lord commanded saying, The fathers shall not die for the children, neither shall the children die for the fathers." He was trying to do right. He was trying to follow the law.

But let's see how his life went. The children of Esau, the Edomites, were continuing to give trouble; they needed to be dealt with. It was right that he should go out and battle against them in this particular time and situation. "He hired also an hundred thousand mighty men of valour out of Israel," from the northern tribes. Verse 6. He hired them for a hundred talents of silver. These soldiers were gathered together, ready to go to battle, when a "man of God" came (verse 7) saying, "O king, let not the army of Israel go with thee; for the Lord is not with Israel." If you go out with Israel, with these hundred thousand extra men, you will fall before your enemy (verse 8). "For God hath power to help, and to cast down." Thus spoke a "man of God" to Amaziah, who served God but not with a complete or whole heart. How would he respond? He didn't do too badly. He only asked a question most of us would have asked. He "said to the man of God, But what shall we do for the hundred talents which I have given to the army of Israel?" Verse 9. These mercenaries were paid in advance, and there were no refunds. Furthermore, they wanted to fight.

Now the man of God said to Amaziah, when he questioned about his money, "The Lord is able to give thee much more than this." And this king, with the divided heart, obeyed and sent the army of Israel home with his hundred talents of silver. "Their anger was greatly kindled against Judah, and they returned home in great anger (verse 10), but Amaziah was courageously unconcerned. He could have done no worse than to tell a mercenary, "Look, I've paid you, but please go home. I don't need you." They were very, very angry. Amaziah knew that, but he obeyed. He lost his money and reduced his army by one fourth. He went out to battle and victory in the name of the Lord. Quite the man, this Amaziah who served the Lord but not with his whole heart. But let's read on.

"It came to pass, that after Amaziah was come from the slaughter of the Edomites, that he brought the gods of the children of Seir," and he was supposed to destroy them. But instead (verse 14) he "set them up to be his gods, and bowed down himself before them, and burned incense to them." Can you imagine that? Had he lost his mind? When he came back from his victory, the prophet came again to him and said (verse 15), "Why hast thou sought after the gods of the people, which could not deliver their own people out of thine hand?" You went out in the name of the Lord of heaven and earth, you obeyed Him, you risked the anger of 100,000 men, you lost a hundred talents of silver, you got much more back, and you won a victory with an army large enough to fight only half the battle. But you took their gods which couldn't protect them from you and set them up to be *your* gods!

Do you think he was insane? Let us be warned, and many of us know it already by experience, that when you serve God without a total, complete surrender, you often find yourself doing some very foolish things, things which shock other people and may even surprise yourself. Now when the prophet asked him about seeking after false gods, Amaziah was obviously embarrassed. "And it came to pass, as he talked with him, that the king said unto him, Art thou made of the king's counsel?" Verse 16. "Who asked you anyway? Keep quiet! Do you want to die? I don't want to hear any more about this." Have you ever felt that way? You've done something wrong; you don't really know why, and you don't want to talk about it?

What now became of Amaziah? Follow the chapter through. His own people "made a conspiracy against him in Jerusalem; and he fled to Lachish: but they sent to Lachish after him, and slew him there." Verse 27. The tragic, inglorious end of a young life. A life that looked promising for a time. But half-surrender turned to total loss and failure. So it will be with anyone who serves God with an incomplete heart.

In Salt Lake City we once rented a home with beautiful floors—highly varnished and waxed. I noticed one day in a corner of the bedroom a small dark brown spot on the floor. As I pushed on the wood around the spot, the entire board collapsed; there was nothing underneath. It had been eaten away by termites. Only a paper-thin veneer of varnish and wax had covered the rotten hollow. The veneer appeared as genuine wood, but so thin you could crumble it like ash.

"Sin is like a termite. It eats away at the heart of the character." I thought again of that floorboard—the last thing to show decay was the exterior. I heard of a person in the deep woods leaning against a dead but large and solid-looking tree only to have it topple. It looked solid enough, but it had been gutted by termites.

That's what happened to Amaziah. He had been hollowed out by cherished sin. We don't know all of his sins. One thing you can be sure of; there was something about the worship of those gods which appealed to his natural, half-surrendered heart. We may wonder at the intelligence of the idolators of Scripture, but there was something in false worship that attracted their sensual, unconverted, unsurrendered hearts. It is doubtful that Amaziah believed the gods of the Edomites were better and stronger than the God whom he knew to be in heaven. Second Kings 17:33 describes a people who "feared the Lord, *and* served their own gods." Perhaps Amaziah was also trying to hang on to both. We do that today—our idols *and* God. We keep back things for ourselves. And this will be our defeat—cherished idols of the soul.

Was everyone at the time of the flood openly evil—murdering, taking by force others' wives, and so forth? Were all so obviously wicked that any observer would have agreed a mass destruction was imperative? This was not the case.

Noah had a rather large "church." His was perhaps the first revival or reform movement clearly identified in Scripture. Noah proclaimed the message of God and offered the only place of promise and protection. And many seemed to recognize much truth in his message and that of the other faithful patriarchs. "The men of that generation were not all, in the fullest acceptance of the term, idolators. Many professed to be worshipers of God." But, interestingly enough, we're told this class was foremost in finally rejecting the preaching of Noah. "As sin became general, it appeared less and less sinful, and they finally declared that the divine law was no longer in force. . . . Had the men of that generation obeyed the divine law, they would have recognized the voice of God in the warning of His servant; but their minds had become so blinded by the rejection of light that they really believed Noah's message to be a delusion."—*Patriarchs and Prophets*, pp. 95, 96.

Have we not been warned that "those who have step by step yielded to worldly demands and conformed to worldly customs will not find it a hard matter to yield to the powers that be, rather than subject themselves to derision, insult, threatened imprisonment, and death"?—*Testimonies*, vol. 5, p. 81. It is not hard to give up a half-faith. I once heard a young man say, "I know I'm not a very good Christian. I know there are many things I should do differently. But when it really comes down to the end, I'll be in there." But will he really? Scripture says he that is unfaithful in that which is least will be unfaithful also in much. Do we think if we're weak when things are easy, we'll be stronger when things are hard? Has Satan somehow deluded us to this extent? Do we really believe we can willfully compromise here or there, hold back this or that, question the principles of Scripture illuminated in the inspired writings and still find ourselves responding to the presence of the loving Saviour during the times of crisis ahead? Will we stand with Christ, faithful even unto death, or will we be pushed on by Satan into total despair and final ruin, as were Judas, Amaziah, and those outside the ark?

Back to the antediluvians as described in *Patriarchs and Prophets*, page 95 and following. Many had obeyed God, but not fully; they had not completely followed God's will. Thus, when Noah spoke they failed even to hear the voice of God. They were arguing with him even before he said anything. Yet "a power attended his [Noah's] words, for it was the voice of God."—Page 96. But by "resistance to the reproofs of conscience and the warnings of God's prophet, that generation filled up the measure of their iniquity, and became ripe for destruction."—Page 97. Remember that these were God-worshipers; they weren't idolators in the sense we might think, probably in no more obvious sense than we are today. They were worshipers of God, and they were listening to Noah's message. But when it came right down to the end of things—to the point of actually leaving everything (in our day, equivalent to walking away from our homes, our cars, our boats, our businesses, and even our families in some instances) and moving into the ark—Noah was asking too much!

"Many at first appeared to receive the warning; yet they did not turn to God with true repentance. They were unwilling to renounce their sins. During the time that elapsed before the coming of the Flood, their faith was tested, and they failed to endure the trial. Overcome by the prevailing unbelief, they finally joined their former associates in rejecting the solemn message. Some were deeply convicted and would have heeded the warning; but there were so many to jest and ridicule, that they partook of the same spirit, resisted the invitations of mercy, and were soon among the boldest and most defiant scoffers; for none are so reckless and go to such lengths in sin as do those who have once had light, but have resisted the convicting Spirit of God."—*Patriarchs and Prophets*, p. 95.

How sad! All those people buried in the floodwaters were obviously not preparing for that kind of grave. Many thought they were preparing to go inside, were listening to Noah, some helping him drive the nails. They may even have been *enthusiastic* about building the boat. But somehow while the building went on, they went home day by day to their own worldly pleasures and treasures and halfhearted way of living. And when the final test came, they found it impossible to enter the ark. Will a similar move be possible for you and me if we do not give God our whole heart today and each day?

A Christian businessman who stopped by our fair-booth display of Christian literature said, "I was never really happy until I put everything on the altar! Until I surrendered everything—my wife, my children, my business [he was a successful businessman]—until I put it all on the altar, I was never happy." It has taken me a number of years to understand what he was talking about. Just married myself, I wasn't sure how one would put wife and children and everything on the altar. But today I'm convinced that's what it really takes. Everything.

We must be *willing* to give up anything and everything, life itself, in order to be on God's side. A total, complete surrender. And this is where we often fail.

"The whole heart must be yielded to God, or the change can never be wrought in us by which we are to be restored to His likeness."—*Steps to Christ*, pp. 43. And further, "Sin however small it may be esteemed, can be indulged in only at the peril of infinite loss. What we do not overcome, will overcome us and work out our destruction." *Steps to Christ*, pp. 32, 33. Not *might*, not *may*, not *perhaps*. "What we do not overcome, *will* overcome us and work out our destruction." We cannot indulge in sin. We are not here talking about the occasional misdeed, but sin *indulged*. A willful act, a decision to harbor what one knows to be wrong. Again, "Even one wrong trait of character, one sinful desire, persistently cherished [please notice "persistently cherished"], will eventually neutralize all the power of the gospel."—*Steps to Christ*, p. 34.

Symptoms of cherished sin may be words or thoughts such as these, "Leave me alone—I know it's wrong, but don't bother me about it." This may be spoken to God directly or in reply to a mother, father, teacher, preacher, husband, wife, or child through whom God seeks to lead you. That which you know is sin, but in which you willfully persist, will eventually destroy completely your relationship with God. That's what happened to Amaziah. That's what happened to Judas. It brought tragedy to the people before the Flood, and half-surrender still brings disaster to a great number of us today. But we *must* not allow it! We must lay all on the altar. That the Father is waiting for such a commitment there can be no doubt. He cannot work in partnership with Satan. How He longs for us to give Him our hearts!

A man in Ogden, Utah, told me a sad story I'll never forget. His daughter, who had been a good girl, grew up, became wayward, got in with the wrong crowd, and soon married a fellow who wasn't much good. They divorced, and she married another who wasn't much better. Another divorce was followed by a third marriage and a third divorce. Still a young woman, she went to Las Vegas to work. You who have children know a father's love doesn't change at times like this. After a few months she wanted to come home. She wrote asking for the bus fare. He sent the money and waited. He left his job at midday to meet the first possible bus that would bring his little girl home. He waited but she didn't come. In the middle of that night he met the only other bus but was disappointed. Each midday and midnight for several days he was at the station. Finally he gave up.

Several months went by. She wrote again, "Dad, I know I disappointed you last time, but this time I'm really coming home. I don't have any money." He sent the money again. The day he thought she'd arrive he was at the bus depot. He waited. At midnight he waited again. Noon again, and midnight. Every day for three or four days. Again he gave up.

After a long while she wrote the third time, "Dad, this time I really mean it. I'm coming home. I'm tired of this life. I'm coming home." Once again the money was sent. He met the noon bus, searched every face. Midnight, the same thing. He sadly gave up and returned to his home. At 4 a.m. the phone rang.

"I'm a friend of your daughter. She bought her ticket and got on the bus—and we talked her out of coming home. She got off the bus and got into our car. We had an accident. Your daughter is dead."

The sad father pointed to a grave we could see from his window. "She's buried there," he said.

The Father is always waiting. Let there be no question about that. What we said in chapter 1 is always true. You can be assured He is waiting with open, eager arms for you and me. You may think that applies only to people outside the church, but He's waiting for many in the church as well. Have we made a total, complete, and full surrender to Him? While He is always waiting, it is a definite possibility that tomorrow will be too late. That isn't said just to frighten you. It's just true. Tomorrow can become too late, either by death or in a more subtle and dangerous way. We can become so hopelessly entangled in sin and compromise, or simply in material things, projects, and plans. All this can take us so far away it becomes impossible for us to turn around and come to Him. Yet you can be assured He is there. He's waiting, and He'll send you "the money." He's paid the price. The ticket has been purchased. Nothing more is required. You need no gift to bring him, but you do need to turn to Him in a complete and genuine surrender of heart and mind and soul.

That's my appeal. Whatever it is that holds you back, whatever it is that you are clinging to—give it all to Him.

Dear Father, we thank You for the great love with which You have loved us. We're thankful this love never changes, that You forever reach out after us. May we today give You our whole hearts. Reveal to us our cherished idols, and may we be willing to surrender them all for a life with you, now and forever. May we not be satisfied with merely being in Your presence, but may we be totally responsive as You constantly unfold Your perfect plan for our lives. We pray in Jesus' name. Amen.

God's Final Question—Whom Do You Worship?

In chapter 2 we were reminded that God cannot save us in parts. He cannot save a segment of you or me. We know the soul is the total being, and when God saves your soul, He saves you. And that means you surrender to Him everything you have and are and represent. You cannot reserve any small part for yourself and expect God to save the rest. "There are some who are seeking, always seeking, for the goodly pearl. But they do not make an entire surrender of their wrong habits. They do not die to self that Christ may live in them. Therefore they do not find the precious pearl. They have not overcome unholy ambition and their love for worldly attractions. They do not lift the cross, and follow Christ in the path of self-denial and self-sacrifice." And the result? "They never know what it is to have peace and harmony in the soul."—*Selected Messages*, bk. 1, pp. 399, 400.

Remember the man who was never really happy until he put everything on the altar? Everything—without reserve. Those who cling to and cherish wrong habits and are unwilling to overcome their unholy ambitions or to surrender their desires for wealth and personal success and worldly pleasure can never experience the joy of salvation. All these ambitions seem so terribly important, yet the fact is that no goals in this life and this world are really important, except as they contribute to our salvation and that of others. We really don't have to experience everything this world offers, do we? Do we really need all of the things that would be nice to possess? A place to live and a vehicle to go about in, perhaps, and a few extra comforts along the way, but are we not willing to exchange even these things for eternity?

This may mean putting even some good things in their proper place. For example, could I make an idol of something so innocent as gardening? Up at 5:00 on summer mornings to make sure you have the best crop in the neighborhood. Not much time to pray and study God's word. The always busy good man or woman can be lost as surely as the slothful sinner. Any pursuit can become an unholy activity if it is carried to extremes. Full surrender is required; even the garden and the kitchen must be God's. The quotation above suggests that without this type of devotion to God and His purposes, there can be no rest, no joy. Many are almost, yet not fully, Christian. They seem near the kingdom of heaven but do not enter. "Almost but not wholly saved means to be not almost but wholly lost."—*Selected Messages*, bk 1, p. 400.

And God is not mean or arbitrary in that declaration, is He? He just knows it can be no other way; He can't save people in fragments. He must have everything. And the rewards of full surrender are tremendous to have peace and joy—even now. What more could one really want? Many of our ambitions are motivated by a desire for peace, joy, satisfaction, and rest. But we are often disappointed, aren't we? The only safe and sure way is to give everything to God. Put all on the altar, and keep it there every day. And He will return all that will contribute genuinely to your present and eternal good. This is so very, very basic and yet so hard for us to grasp. Of too many of us it can be said, as was declared of the mixed worship of the Samaritans, "They feared the Lord, *and* served their own gods, . . . both their children, and their children's children: as did their fathers, so do they unto this day." 2 Kings 17:33-41.

But this will never do; God and His will must always have unrivaled priority in our lives. "Thou shalt worship the Lord thy God, and him only shalt thou serve," said Jesus. Matthew 4:10.

Idolatry comes in forms hardly recognizable as such. When Christ arrived on earth, idolatry in the Old Testament sense was no longer a problem for Israel. They had been effectively cured of serving the gods of the heathen by the Babylonian captivity many years before. Though surrounded by idol worshipers, the Palestinian Jews of Christ's day abhorred idolatry. They were not, however, delivered from Satan's subtle temptations. It is often true that a little time after the world is given up, we lose our first love and devotion to God—our first gratitude for His acceptance of us. The enemy then tempts us to make an idol of our own religion.

That's the condition the Jews were in when Jesus arrived on earth. They were idolaters, but in a new way. They were very religious. And Satan had succeeded quite generally in seducing them to become self-centered, turning from the idolatry of the world to idolizing their own religious ceremonies. As was true of ancient Israel, they "kept not the commandments of the Lord their God, but walked in the statutes of Israel which they made." 2 Kings 17:19. They taught "for doctrines the commandments of men." Matthew 15:9. In the time of Christ many of Israel did keep the commandments in a sense. They guarded the Sabbath meticulously and observed many other commandments and traditions. And they thought they were doing very well. They were ever searching for more things they might do to please God and earn His favor. They failed to truly worship God as their Deliverer, trusting rather to their own works.

Now let's turn to Revelation 13 and 14 and see what God's last-day message has to say about undivided worship of the Creator and Redeemer. You know, of course, those two chapters contain the three angels' messages; the whole issue in the final scenes of the great controversy will center around those messages. Ellen White asserted that those three angel voices proclaim the call to righteousness by faith. This perplexes some of us. Let's see if we can discover the basic issues.

One thing we must notice from the beginning is that in these chapters Satan works in a religious, even Christian, guise. Satan doesn't always clothe himself in his own true robes. Unfortunately, wherever God is named and professed and worshiped, we come to expect only God and not Satan to be present. So let's remember that Satan is often carefully concealed in the robes of an angel of light and that the conflict often cannot be easily discerned as a controversy between Christ and Satan.

In chapter 13 we interpret the dragon to be primarily Satan and secondarily pagan Rome. (See Revelation 12 where the dragon was waiting to devour the man child that was born to the woman.) You will notice (verse 4) that this dragon was worshiped. Let us focus our attention on the word *worship* in Revelation 13 and 14. These chapters concern themselves with this basic issue—whom are we really worshiping? Where do we place our trust? Under the symbol of the dragon there was the worship of heathen deities and the emperor. In the coliseums of pagan Rome countless numbers of Christians were sacrificed for refusing to pay homage to the gods of Rome. Pagan Rome believed the worship of Jesus Christ to be a threat to the empire. As a test of loyalty Roman citizens were required on pain of death to burn incense to the emperor. Some Roman citizens who were Christians compromised. While lifting their eyes to the God of heaven, they placed a pinch of incense on Caesar's altar, flattering themselves that they burned incense only with the hand while they worshiped God with the mind. Because they served God, and also "served their graven images" (2 Kings 17:41), they lived, while those totally loyal to Christ who refused to burn incense to a deified Caesar, died.

This dragon gave his power to the beast. The beast (verse 4) also was worshiped. "Who is like unto the beast?" came the question. "Who is able to make war with him?" "And all that dwell upon the earth shall *worship* him, whose names are not written in the book of life of the Lamb slain" Verse 8. We have here brought to view a religious power, a Christian body, the most visibly identifiable Christian body on earth, the Christian church. Much of pagan Rome had become Christian, and in the process Christianity had become dangerously pagan. In A.D. 533 the emperor Justinian declared the bishop of Rome the head of all Christian churches, accelerating the Roman church's rise to power. Both within and without this body were Christ's true followers, many who paid with their lives for heeding conscience and Scripture rather than worshiping the church and her dogmas.

The change in God's church had come subtly, gradually—a trust in ceremonies and human intercession, in making pilgrimages, in adoring relics and images, and then in the actual sale of indulgences. Indulgences could at times be earned by fighting in a "holy war" against non-Christian nations. Man's actions were accepted by the church as meritorious. Indulgences were in the first place available on the basis of the excess merits of the saints, so said the church, and now others could share in these earned merits by works of their own which the church declared acceptable. We referred in chapter 1 to indulgences even today being offered for the reading of Scripture. This is all out of harmony with God's plan of salvation in which remission of sins is based solely on the merits of Christ and His sacrifice.

This was Luther's concern when he nailed his ninety-five theses on the church door at Wittenberg. He really loved the church and wanted to see it reformed. He had no desire or intention to leave. At that point if anyone had told him he was going to give up the priesthood and lead much of Roman Catholic Europe out of his church, he wouldn't have believed them. He only wanted her to teach the true way of salvation. All of the ninety-five theses were concerned with one subject—the doctrine of indulgences. In the main they declared that man cannot earn or purchase his salvation or any part of the favor of God by his own acts, whatever the church may declare. Nothing man can do can earn the favor of God. This is only a brief glimpse of the false worship under the beast's power.

Revelation (chapter 13, verse 11) brings to view a harmless-appearing beast coming up out of the earth. It has two horns like a lamb, but later it speaks as a dragon. "He exerciseth all the power of the first beast before him, and causeth the earth and them which dwell therein to *worship* the first beast, whose deadly wound was healed." Verse 12. This new beast now "doeth great wonders" (verse 13), making "fire come down from heaven on the earth in the sight of men." And he deceives the world by means of "miracles" and causes "that as many as would not *worship the image of the beast* should be killed. And he causeth all, both small and great, rich and poor, free and bond, to receive a mark in their right hand, or in their foreheads," and to receive "the number of his name." Verses 14-17.

Notice how the word *worship* has repeatedly arisen: *worship* the dragon, *worship* the beast, *worship* the image of the beast. All false worshipers finally receive a name, a mark, a number in their hands or in their foreheads. Now the contrast. John looked again, "and, lo, a Lamb stood on the mount Sion." This is a true lamb, not a beast with horns like a lamb. This is the Lamb of God standing "on the mount Sion, and with him an hundred forty and four thousand, having his Father's name written in their foreheads." Revelation 14:1. You will notice it is *the Father's name* in the foreheads of this group not the name or mark of the beast. Also there is no provision for this mark to be placed in the hand. The worship of God must be, and can only truly be, with the whole mind and heart. One can worship the beast halfheartedly, merely conforming and submitting to its demands. But God must have you totally. In the hand only, will not do. The Father's name must be in the forehead, which represents your total being.

This group has responded to the call of the three angels of chapter 14. The thirteenth and fourteenth chapters of Revelation must be studied together. The word *worship* continues to arise. Verses 7, 9, 11. These angels have called God's children away from the false worship of Babylon, away from the worship of "the beast and his image" to complete worship and trust in the saving power of the Creator-Redeemer. This is the "everlasting gospel." Verse 6. This is righteousness by faith. Salvation has never been on any other terms. Fear God and give glory to *Him*, for He's the One who will judge you. Give glory to and worship Him only who can save. Don't worship the beast; there is no salvation there. Don't worship the dragon; don't worship the image of the beast; don't worship any of the fallen Babylonian systems of religion. Don't submit to any national efforts to somehow earn the favor of God by whatever man-enforced laws, whether a Sunday law or a Sabbath law (both have been suggested by Christian leaders of recent times). Attempts to make people religious by mere churchly acts and ceremonies always create a worship of something or someone other than God. "Fear God, and give glory to *Him*, . . . and worship *Him* that made heaven, and earth, and the sea, and the fountains of waters." Verse 7.

Observance of the true Sabbath, given by God at creation and strongly suggested in the first angel's message (verses 6, 7), was ever intended to be a sign of our total trust in the saving power of our Creator and Redeemer. (Exodus 31:13; Ezekiel 20:20). It is possible, however, to keep the Sabbath in an idolatrous way today, just as did Israel in Jesus' time. Let's remember the reasons we keep the Sabbath. We are to keep it holy, all of it, the edges too. We're to guard each moment as precious but for one purpose—and that is to worship God. The Sabbath is not a day to demonstrate our superior goodness. Quite the opposite. The Sabbath is a weekly reminder that our trust must *not* be in ourselves, not be in anything we can do, including our Sabbath keeping. It must symbolize and actually be a time of total trust in that God who made us in the beginning and who only can save us and create us anew.

Sabbath keeping has been commanded to tear us loose once each week from even some good things of life which can rob us of eternity. When the sun sets and you know that Sabbath has come, what a load of legitimate cares lifts off the shoulders of the true Sabbath keeper. Concerns about schoolwork, about the house you're building, about taxes, and about pressures at your job will roll away, because you know this is holy time, a time to worship God, a time to give Him glory and to devote oneself in a special way to Him and His creatures.

We must ever beware that our religion does not become a mere form and keep us from God. It is possible to come to church and not worship. Have you had that experience? Perhaps your mind was on many other things and not at all tuned to God and His word, not at all sensitive to the calls of his Spirit. It is possible to get the idea there is some merit in putting in your time attending meetings. In all our religiosity let's remember we don't worship our religion, we don't worship the Sabbath. We worship God. The call of the hour is to "fear God, and give glory to him: . . . and worship Him that made heaven, and earth, and the sea, and the fountains of waters."

Our Father, we thank You for the message of the three angels, reminding us that in You we live and move and have our being and that in You we must put our trust if we will ever be saved. We trust You for our salvation, and we ask

You to not only write our names above and keep them written there, but to write Your holy name in our foreheads. May we be among that group, worshiping the Lamb and having Your name written in our very minds and hearts.

Father, point out to us our idols; show us wherein we are still trusting in anything other than You, whether it be in the world, in the church, or in our own religious experience. May we learn what it means to worship You and to trust you totally for anything and everything, here and now, and for eternity. We pray in Jesus' name. Amen.

Your Trials—Harmful or Helpful?

Let us review briefly. God's love, ability, willingness and almost impatient eagerness to save us could be summed up in Jesus' grief over unresponsive Jerusalem. "How often would I have gathered thy children together, as a hen doth gather her brood under her wings, *and ye would not.*" Luke 13:34. "With a yearning heart, Jesus saw those who had been His disciples departing from Him, the Life and the Light of men. The consciousness that His compassion was unappreciated, His love unrequited, His mercy slighted, His salvation rejected, filled Him with sorrow that was inexpressible."—*The Desire of Ages*, p. 393.

Jesus is reaching out after us; let us never question that fact. He longs to gather us under His wings. He yearns after us, though very conscious that His compassion for us is often unappreciated, His love not responded to, His mercy slighted. And this ultimately adds up to the rejection of salvation. This fills Him with a sorrow that is inexpressible. Even as He wept over Jerusalem, so He weeps over us and for the same reason—we won't let Him save us. He wants to, He attempts to, He's eager to, He's more than able, and we "would not." The only limitation to God's saving power is our unwillingness to respond.

When we are not wholly under the control of God, we are under the control of Satan. Though it sometimes seems so, there is really no halfway place in this matter. We are in effect wholly for God or wholly for Satan. We are deceived when we think we can have a little of both. Many have tried to serve God with a divided heart, and with tragic results. As we fail fully to trust and obey Christ, we effectively surrender to His enemy, and ours. "Whosoever abideth in him sinneth not." . . . "He that committeth sin is of the devil." 1 John 3:6, 8. "The tempter can never compel us to do evil. He cannot control minds unless they are yielded to his control. The will must consent, faith must let go its hold upon Christ, before Satan can exercise his power upon us. But every sinful desire we cherish affords him a foothold."—*The Desire of Ages*, p. 125.

Do we afford Satan a foothold by holding back just a little from God? Satan does not need a very big hold, does he? He seems to be an excellent climber. Have you watched a skillful rock-climber? He seems to walk straight up bare rock on invisible toeholds. A few years ago a man climbed without equipment up the side of one of the tallest buildings in the world in New York City. The dumbfounded and securely scaffolded window washers asked him, "Where are you going?" He replied, "I'm going for a walk!" Satan is similarly skilled in conquering even the tallest Christians. He only requires a toehold at some low spot to make rapid progress. And so, "every sinful desire we cherish affords him a foothold." Satan will make the best of the openings we give him. Every point at which we willfully fail to meet the divine standard is an open door by which he can enter to tempt and destroy.

"God leads His people on, step by step. He brings them up to different points calculated to manifest what is in the heart. Some endure at one point, but fall off at the next."—*Testimonies*, vol. 1, p. 187. And that's the way it is at times. We are successful at one point; at the next we fail. "At every advanced point the heart is tested and tried a little closer. . . . Some are willing to receive one point; but when God brings them to another testing point, they shrink from it and stand back, because they find that it strikes directly at some cherished idol."—*Ibid.* Please notice—*cherished* idol. "Here they have opportunity to see what is in their hearts that shuts out Jesus."—*Ibid.* Whenever we resist His knock at our hearts and shut out Jesus, even in what seems a small matter, we invite Satan in. And he needs just a toehold. Each time we *cherish* an idol, just a little one, even though professing to be Christians—each attempt we make to serve God and also our graven images (2 Kings 17:41)—we open the door for Satan to come in. And so we shut out Jesus; we "prize something higher than the truth" and our "hearts are not prepared to receive Jesus."—*Ibid.*

Mercifully, "individuals are tested and proved *a length of time* to see if they will sacrifice their idols and heed the counsel of the True Witness. If any will not be purified through obeying the truth, and overcome their selfishness, their pride, and evil passions, the angels of God have the charge: 'They are joined to their idols, let them alone.' [See Hosea 4:17.]"—*Ibid.* Emphasis Supplied. It is important to remember we are here discussing Christians, the people of God, who perhaps have only small idols they try to bring along with them into the presence of God. After "a length of time," it is declared, " 'they are joined to their idols, let them alone,' and they [the angels] pass on to their work, leaving these with their sinful traits unsubdued, to the control of evil angels."—*Ibid.* What a thought! When we put ourselves out of Christ by failing to surrender fully, we put ourselves under the control of evil angels! But "those who come up to every point, and stand every test, and overcome, be the price what it may, have heeded the counsel of the True Witness, and they will receive the latter rain, and thus be fitted for translation."—*Ibid.*

A multitude of subtle temptations to idolatry and self-worship will plague at times everyone reading these lines. Satan will tempt in every possible way to take the attention off God, off Christ, our only hope of salvation, and put it on something else. If he cannot discourage us with our failures, if he cannot distract us by the things of the world, if we've sacrificed every material thing, and it seems some have, then he may attempt to place our focus on our own "humility," our own self-sacrifice, our own prayers, our own faithfulness. In this way we are conquered, because we once again look to self instead of to Him. Our trust is not in prayer; we trust in God. We trust not in faith; we trust in God. How quickly Satan steals in upon the heels of an experience of faith, a time when the Lord has heard our helpless cry. There he is congratulating us for our faith. "My, if everyone had a faith like yours!" Salvation or deliverance of any kind is not by our faith, but by our Christ, in whom we place our unmeritorious, helpless trust. In fact, every Christian duty we perform, whether it be giving tithes and offerings, whether it be healthful care of our bodies, whether it be baptism or the Lord's Supper or feet washing—all must be a manifestation of trust *in Him* or acts to bring us into a deeper and more constant abiding in Him. Never must we allow Christian responsiveness, Christian duty and obedience, or Christian worship to be turned back upon ourselves, as though we are doing something great which has purchasing power with God. The call of the hour is to "fear *God*, and give glory *to Him*" and to "*worship him.*" Revelation 14:7.

Now to the subject of this chapter—are your trials harmful or helpful? Are we in danger of losing our souls over the happenings in a sinful world which God allows to touch our lives and the lives of others? Even good Christians will at times come very near to doubting God's goodness because of the trials that come to other people and to themselves. Now you may think you've heard enough of this subject before, but please listen once more. We're going to discuss one of the strangest and most enlightening stories of the Old Testament.

But first to Hebrews 12. "Wherefore seeing we also are compassed about with so great a cloud of witnesses, let us lay aside every weight, and the sin which doth so easily beset us, and let us run with patience the race that is set before us, looking unto Jesus the author and finisher of our faith." Verses 1, 2. Why are we being asked to look to Jesus? In the context, the author of Hebrews is setting forth Jesus' sufferings and humiliation as an example and encouragement to His followers who were being severely tried. "For the joy that was set before him," Jesus "endured the cross," not considering the shame worthy of notice that He might victoriously sit "down at the right hand of the throne of God." Next the Hebrews are invited to "consider him who endured from sinners such hostility against himself." Verse 3, RSV. Why are they asked to consider this? "Lest ye be wearied and faint in your minds." "For whom the Lord loveth he chasteneth, and scourgeth every son whom he receiveth." Verses 3, 6. This counsel was available to them in the Hebrew proverbs of Solomon. (See Proverbs 3:11, 12.) The Hebrews are now further reminded, "Ye have not resisted unto blood, striving against sin." Verse 4. And if you are reading this book, the same can be said of you. This was not intended as a guarantee that Christ's followers would not have to make the supreme sacrifice—to partake of Christ's sufferings to this extent. Indeed some had in the past (chapter 11:35-37), and some of them would be martyred in the near future. This is the very point being made: We should be willing to give all for the kingdom, even as Christ gave all for us. The Hebrews are mildly reproved because they had "forgotten the exhortation which speaketh unto you as unto children, My son, despise not thou the chastening of the Lord, nor faint when thou art rebuked of Him." Verse 5.

It's much easier to write about this matter of relating properly to trial than it is to believe what you have written when you are undergoing trial yourself. We can tell people how they should relate to their troubles, but when perplexing, disappointing experiences come to us it's different, isn't it? Trials seldom come in the same form to two people. At times we believe we can see clearly why others are tested; after all it's plain they needed it! But when difficulties and disasters, griefs and heartaches overtake us, we cry out, "Why *me*, Lord? Haven't I been faithful?" But our heavenly Father makes no mistakes in dealing with His children, unlike earthly fathers (see verses 9, 10), who can have tainted motives and feelings when administering even necessary punishment. We can be assured when God chastens it is always "for our profit, that we might be partakers of His holiness" (verse 10), and not the least tainted with sadism, vindictiveness, or even pride and embarrassment. If we will "let God be true" (Romans 3:4), then the person who said recently, "I think God hates me," because of the sadnesses which have come into his life, must be wrong.

A final word from Hebrews 12 and we will go to our interesting and enlightening story in the book of Judges. "Now no chastening for the present seemeth to be joyous, but grievous: nevertheless afterward it yieldeth the peaceable fruit of righteousness unto them which are exercised thereby. Wherefore lift up the hands which hang down, and the feeble knees; and make straight paths for your feet." Verses 11-13.

Now to Judges. These were the days when "every man did that which was right in his own eyes." Judges 17:6. A very sordid crime had been committed in the tribe of Benjamin (Chapter 19). The other tribes in Israel felt Benjamin should be willing to submit to some discipline or at least to some inquiry into the terrible deed done. But Benjamin proved unwilling to assist in bringing the criminals to justice (Chapter 20:13). A confrontation seemed imminent. "The children of Benjamin gathered themselves together out of the cities unto Gibeah, to go out to battle against the children of Israel." Benjamin could boast "twenty and six thousand men that drew sword, beside the inhabitants of Gibeah [the city where the crime took place], which were numbered seven hundred chosen men." Among Benjamin's army "were seven hundred chosen men left-handed; every one could sling stones in an hair breadth, and not miss." Verses 14-16. An unusual group indeed, and peculiarly skillful in combat. Nonetheless they were badly outnumbered, for the army of the tribes of Israel gathered against Benjamin "numbered four hundred thousand men that drew sword: all these were men of war." Verse 17.

Despite the odds in their favor, Israel knew it was a serious matter to war against their own brethren, so they "arose, and went up to the house of God, and asked counsel of God, and said, Which of us shall go up first to the battle against the children of Benjamin? And the Lord said, Judah shall go up first." So among all the tribes of Israel, Judah was clearly instructed to go up first to the battle. And what happened? Surely a great victory for Judah, because they went to battle at the command of God. Let's see: "And the children of Israel. . . went out to battle against Benjamin; and . . . put themselves in array to fight against them at Gibeah." And what happened? They had asked counsel of God and God had told them to go out and fight. "And the children of Benjamin came forth out of Gibeah, and destroyed down to the ground of the Israelites that day twenty and two thousand men." Verses 19-21. So that's what you get when you ask God's counsel and He tells you to go fight! Strange isn't it? They lost 22,000 men!

The trial was severe, but did God know with what kind of people He was dealing? Does God ever test His children above that which they are able to bear? How did Judah react? "And the men of Israel encouraged themselves, and set their battle again in array in the place where they had put themselves in array the first day." They weren't quitting yet, nor did they fail to seek the Lord's guidance. They "went up and wept before the Lord until even, and asked counsel of the Lord." Notice that they not only asked counsel, but they also wept before the Lord. They asked, "Shall I go up again to battle against the children of Benjamin my brother?" Could that be the problem? Should they be fighting against their brother Benjamin at all? They wanted to know. The counsel of God was clear, "The Lord said, Go up against him." Verses 22, 23. "The children of Israel came near against the children of Benjamin the second day. And Benjamin went forth against them out of Gibeah the second day, and destroyed down to the ground of the children of Israel again eighteen thousand men." Verses 24, 25. The second day they had wept before the Lord and again asked His counsel, and they were defeated! Where is their God? What kind of God is this? Surely there's some mistake!

Do you see any parallels in your own experiences? Do you also have times when you think you've prayed enough, when you've been humbled enough, when you believe you're willing, when you feel you've learned enough already of whatever lesson God is trying to teach you? You ask God's counsel, you weep before Him, and He seems to let you down again? Christian workers—literature evangelists, youth leaders, teachers, missionaries, parents—have you ever asked, "Shall I try again? Yesterday was bad. Shall I stay with it, or shall I quit?" The answer seems clear: "Go back to the battle." So you go, and the second day is little better than the first.

Let's go back to our story. Was this the end of Israel's efforts to correct rebellious Benjamin? As we said, God knew with whom He was dealing; He knew he had some children here who needed help. Benjamin needed discipline, yes, and God was going to see that he got what he needed. But in the process He was not going to lose the souls of the rest of Israel. He would help them too. And while it seemed the ones who should be losing were triumphant over Israel, they really weren't. Everyone was winning together. Wouldn't that be hard to believe after losing 22,000 the first day and 18,000 the second day?

That's 40,000 now, and more than Benjamin had altogether in fighting men!

So what did Israel do? "Then all the children of Israel, and all the people, went up and came unto the house of God, and wept, and they sat there before the Lord, and fasted that day until even, and offered burnt offerings and peace offerings" (verse 26). You can be assured these were not just offerings to appease God. It seems clear these were genuine heart offerings, admitting they were sinners, that they were in great spiritual need. And they really were, without doubt, in greater need than they could even realize. These were days, as we noted earlier, when every man was doing what was right in his own eyes. The Benjamites were not the only sinners among Israel. They were all sinners, and they all needed to have the discipline and chastening of the Lord.

With each defeat Israel had pressed a little closer to their God. The first time they had asked counsel.The second time they had wept and asked counsel. The third time all the people had come to the house of God. They wept, they waited before the Lord, they fasted that day until evening, they offered burnt offerings and peace offerings before the Lord. With this deep and unanimous spiritual preparation, they once more (verses 27, 28), with the most heartfelt humility, "enquired of the Lord, . . . saying, Shall I yet again go out to battle against the children of Benjamin my brother, or shall I cease?" All self-confidence had fled, even though they had 400,000 men and Benjamin only 26,000. No more did they feel assured of victory in the battle. Conversely, it was to them clearly evident they would lose again without some very special intervention. They recognized the battle was the Lord's and not their own. With this new type of total humility and submission, they had asked for guidance once again. "And the Lord said, Go up; for to morrow I will deliver them into thine hand." Verse 28.

If we read the remainder of this story, we will find they

did all they could to fight the battle well. They cooperated. They did not sit back and do nothing. But they now knew if they were ever going to win, it was the Lord who would add success to their well-organized efforts. This is the lesson we need to learn. While our efforts are important, they are of no value apart from the blessing of God. We must do nothing alone. We must do something but never alone. They had totally given up their self-confidence and fully knew they were merely an instrument of God. The tables now turned; the victory was complete. They "destroyed of the Benjamites that day twenty and five thousand and an hundred men: all these drew the sword. So the children of Benjamin saw that they were smitten." Verses 35, 36.

Benjamin was disciplined, but in the process, so was all Israel. God wants to pour out the abundance of blessings on all his children, and especially His workers, but He will not let them lose their own souls while trying to save someone else's. This is one reason why, even in the work of the Lord, things do not always go smoothly. God is too wise to allow things to go so well we will become self-confident and proud. God knows what we have need of. He knows what we can endure. He knows that for which we are ready and from which we can learn something. Often He will first try to awaken us to grateful worship by giving us an abundance of blessing, by showering us with good things. If these blessings are unappreciated and serve to separate us from God in self-confidence and pride, He then often removes these very blessings and allows us to undergo various trials. He hopes, of course, that we will turn to him and recognize from whence our previous blessings came.

It is not God's purpose that we suffer a great deal of pain, disappointment, deprivation, and grief. He has no pleasure in the suffering of any. We can be certain that, even as a good earthly father does not enjoy punishing his children, God has no joy in seeing us hurt. Would not God be pleased if we, just as a mother hopes for her child, would respond to His counsel, would listen to His word, would find out from the trials and sufferings of others, rather than having to experience pain ourselves? Could we not all avoid some heartaches by devoting ourselves to the Lord faithfully, fully, completely, and by learning from the example of the Bible characters, by learning from witnessing other people's lives? We may fail to respond to gentler methods. But God, you can be sure, loves us too much to let us be lost if He sees that suffering now may help us avoid greater pain in the future and even eternal loss.

I once knew a Christian worker who withheld a faithful tithe for some time. He continued to have success in his work. He felt justified in continuing to rob God and other people to whom he failed to pay his debts, because he felt he had evidence the Lord was blessing him. And it did appear God was still with him in his labors. Often God continues to shower us with blessings even while we're living in sin. Young people, and those older, have been known to justify immoral living because God seemed not to leave them. God does not leave us easily. He hopes by continued kindness, when we are doing things that are hurting Him, ourselves, and others, to awaken our consciences. He hopes we will finally realize how very loving and good a Father He is and that we'll turn to him in gratitude and lay aside all things that are hurting him, and His children, including ourselves.

But if this approach fails, He may suddenly withhold good things, as a parent from a child. A parent may say, "If you can't handle the privileges we've given you in a responsible manner, then we will have to remove them until you appreciate them more." This sometimes works, doesn't it? Sometimes parents have success; sometimes God has success. But other times, even though pride and boastfulness and self-confidence vanish, gratitude and submission to God's better plan do not follow. Instead there is bitterness. We feel God doesn't like us, that He doesn't care, that He's against us. And how that must break His heart! First He has done everything good and kind and gentle, and that has driven us away from Him into self-confidence and pride and earthliness. Next He merely removes a few of those things we call good; and instead of waking up, we become rebellious, resentful and discouraged, questioning his love and often His very existence. How frustrating to a parent when he gets a similar reaction from a child. Does God also feel frustrated at times in His efforts to reach us and to woo us to a loving, free response to him and to His love, His mercy, and His goodness?

We may ask, "Why does not God tell us more clearly what He is trying to do for us? Can He expect a right response from us when we only have a general statement that "all things work together for good"? Could He not be more specific? Let me ask you parents, Is it always possible to make a child understand why he is being restrained, deprived, or punished, even when the reason is crystal clear in your mind and there is absolutely no doubt your requirements are just? Let me illustrate.

When one of our sons was two years old, he developed a habit, exciting to him, but terrifying to his parents. His practice was to run across the rather well-trafficked street in front of our home. Try as we might we could not convince his normal but very young mind that streets are dangerous places, that cars can harm and kill. When we thought the problem was solved, again he would find his way through the garden fence into the street. He had never seen anyone hit by a car, not even a dog. So I made my last desperate attempt at reason, explaining again with all the clarity I could muster, "You're going to get hurt. The cars will run over you; they will kill you." (I began to identify with God in His efforts at communication with us. He knows we understand only a few words, and He attempts to speak to us in whatever words and concepts we can grasp. We may wish the Bible would tell us more about

God and His ways, but could it be He has told us already more than we can understand?) And so after this final effort to explain fully and clearly what would be the inevitable result if he continued his forays into the traffic, he decided it was now time to tell me he had it all worked out—I need not worry. He looked up at me with what I judged to be a rather disgusted look, and explained, "Dad, there aren't any cars; I just shut my eyes and run!" He appeared totally convinced it worked just that way. To his two-year-old mind, when he shut his eyes all the dangers disappeared; what he couldn't see couldn't hurt him.

But besides this "logic " he had on his side the test of experience. He had done it many times, and it always worked. Some have, perhaps wrongly, called this the pragmatic test—if it works, it must be OK. If I can sell Christian literature without paying tithe, it must be safe to withhold tithe. If God blesses me, if He still seems to work in my heart, if I still feel His blessing when I go to church, then God must not care too much about this thing some would call sin. You see, our reason, like that of a child, may be mixed up and immature. The mind of my two-year-old could not grasp that though the cars disappeared from his sight, they were still there. Furthermore, he had tried his belief numbers of times and had always been successful.

Reason had now reached its limit. Pain, punishment, trial, if you please, now took over, administered by a kind but very concerned father who would rather have a bewildered but obedient and living son than one who had unfettered freedom until the moment of his destruction. What would you think of a father who would say, "Well, do your thing, Son," at a time like this? My love demanded that I keep him out of the street—by chastening, not by reason or explanation. Whether he understood or not, I loved him enough to keep him from being struck down by a car or truck. Severity and firmness saved him until he was old enough to comprehend that even the chastening was a manifestation of my love for him and not of my hatred.

God at times chastens us, even severely, before we are "old enough" to grasp why He is doing it. And He'll even risk being hated a little while, if need be, in order to bring us finally to safety and success and eternal life.

It's easy, and common, when we are older, to look back and laugh at our stupidity when we felt our parents were unduly concerned about us, when they were severe beyond what we then thought reasonable. Now we thank them, at times even wishing they'd been a bit harder on us in some areas. But at the time, how hard it is to understand. How angry and frustrated we become. How we wish to be free and wish that parents would be always "loving and helpful" rather than making life so difficult.

So with later trials which God permits. That which we look back upon as a great blessing was, at the time, more pain, disappointment, heartache, and despair than blessing. An accident which brings us near death, brings us also very near to God and makes us forever grateful that He can prepare us for death and give us peace and assurance in His pardoning love. In the backward look, the pain, inconvenience, and bodily scars seem as nothing in comparison. But how seldom we grasp this, even by faith, when we are in the very midst of the trial.

Our extremity is truly God's opportunity, but how rarely can we endure this long in faith! How often we believe our extremity has come sometime before the tide of trial and delay has reached it highest limit.

I recall one such experience when attempting to sell a home. Had we sold our home in the first month of its listing, we would have considered the transaction normal. But as God arranged things, the disposal of this home will forever be a precious chapter in our Christian experience. Six months had elapsed with no buyers, not even any offers or serious inquiries. We'd done all we could: listings with realtors, newspaper and church paper advertisments, open house on successive Sundays, posters directing the way from the main street—all to no apparent avail.

Not until the final day, the latest possible day which would allow us time to move and get settled, did we receive even an offer. By this time we had talked much to the Lord. Did He really want us to move? If so, was not August 16 the last day we could change our mind about the move? It seemed so. Was our price right? We agreed on an exact minimum figure. We felt somehow at peace, realizing even with our best efforts, all was in the Lord's hands. We now awaited developments with a sense of excitement. If no sale, we would stay where we were. We placed all our plans at His feet, willing to give them up or carry them out as His providence would indicate.

After we had waited for six months, August 16 dawned without a single prospective buyer—not one who called us, not even one we could call. Then the phone rang. A woman who had been watching our plight offered an amount within $500 of our minimum figure, not a large discrepancy when dealing with a home. I heard myself telling her kindly that we would have to stay with our price. She replied, "I guess we can't do business then," and hung up. I felt a mild panic; the first and only offer in six months, and on the last day possible, and I was quibbling over $500! Somehow the panic was only momentary, and peace returned along with the belief that either God would provide the full amount or we would know we should not sell at this time. We had been explicit in our prayers as to both date and price.

Two hours later another call from a totally new prospect, and the house was sold for the full figure on that same August 16th! That afternoon, the woman who had phoned earlier that day called to see if we had weakened. Our reply, "The house has been sold," was still almost as dumbfounding to me as it seemed to be to her!

It was a precious experience which still causes us to rejoice. During the anguish of those six months were days when we thought the Lord had forgotten, when He seemed far away, not even on speaking terms with us, at least on the topic of real estate. Those are the hard times, aren't they?

Let us add an important warning here: *Do not expect two experiences to be identical.* It is seldom possible to rely on your own past experience or the experience of someone else as indicative of the details of the next trial in your life. God deals with us as with children, and no two children respond in exactly the same way; and seldom is it necessary to repeat really effective discipline in the same way even with the same child. So when *you* have a house to sell, and the next time we do, the whole experience will very likely be quite different.

For example, in an earlier instance our next-door neighbor had an invitation to a new place of service. Telling no one, the family prayed Sabbath evening, "Lord, if You want us to go, please send us a buyer for our home." Almost immediately after prayer, someone who knew nothing of their situation phoned and asked if perchance they were interested in selling!

How delighted we were to have heard this story when a few months later we also received a call to a new post. We tried an approach similar to that of our former neighbor. So certain were we that we should accept the new assignment and that our home would also sell soon, that we made a deposit on another home. This time no sale came until we had decided not to settle firmly in our new place. We rented instead, wondering why Providence had directed thus. Not many months later, just after gaining much-needed experience in this assignment, we were called to overseas service. A new home at that time in that area would have, we felt later, been just enough to complete our rationalizations for staying in the homeland, which we came near to doing anyway. And what a blessing we would have missed.

Beware. God knows *you*, He knows *me*, He knows what each of us needs and at what time. He deals with us as with children. (See Hebrews 12:9.) Each person and each circumstance demands a slightly different treatment. He does not have the same plans for all of us; hence trials and difficulties, often the Father's teaching and guiding agencies, will vary from person to person and from place to place. This is one reason we must live by faith and trust in our Father, who does all things well for His children.

Let's close this chapter with the text with which we began. "Now no chastening for the present seemeth to be joyous, but grievous: nevertheless *afterward* it yieldeth the peaceable fruit of righteousness unto them which are exercised thereby. Wherefore [and that's my message to everyone of you who are enduring trials of any and every kind] lift up the hands which hang down, and the feeble knees; and make straight paths for your feet." Hebrews 12:11-13.

God is trying to lead you. He wants to lead you. He *is* leading you. He *is* loving you, even through the discipline and the trials and the disappointments that seem so unbearable at times.

Our Father, we do love You and believe You love us. Forgive us when we complain about the trials which You allow. Please continue, despite our lack of understanding, to do what is best for us. We want to be in Your kingdom. By Your grace, we will not give up, be the price what it may. When we finally reach the eternal shores, surely we will declare with one voice, "Heaven is cheap enough!" We long for that day. In Jesus' name we pray. Amen.

God's Church—Do You Belong?

Thus far we have discussed God's love from several perspectives. First, He fully and freely loves and pardons the sinner who turns to Him in faith. Second, He is able to keep forever only those who continue to seek to make an unreserved surrender to Him. Third, He in loving mercy clearly commands that we worship Him and Him only—the source of our lives and our present and eternal salvation. And fourth, knowing the strength of our earthly ties and the subtlety of satanic delusions, He, if need be, uses the severest trials to wrest us from the clutches of Satan and this lost world, in order that we might be forever free from trial and bondage, living eternally in the earth made new.

In this chapter we will explore how our relationship to a loving God involves the church on earth. Does God have a visible church on earth with which the enlightened Christian will identify?

Some of us live in lands where criticism of the leaders of the country seems to be viewed as a mark of intelligence or perception. Who the president is does not seem to matter; to be politically wise, one cannot be too laudatory and unreservedly supportive. This attitude may be carried into the church. Do we think we have an obligation to discover faults in the church, especially in its leadership? Have we come to feel that such keenness of perception is commendable? By this time you have doubtless discovered it unnecessary to look very far or deeply to find faults in anyone and everything. Whether in the church or outside, our world is rather less than perfect. God's church on earth is, without question, "enfeebled and defective," presently, in the past, and as long as she remains on earth.—*Testimonies to Ministers*, p. 49.

In this chapter, however, our emphasis will be that despite the ever-present and apparent defects, His church on earth is the one object on which Christ bestows His supreme regard.—*Ibid*. It would seem if God and Christ bestow upon the church their supreme regard, we would be wise in taking a similar attitude. To like what God likes seems not a bad idea; to cherish and uphold what God cherishes and upholds seems a part of being "laborers together with God."

Does God have a church on earth with which we need concern ourselves at all? We live in an age when it is not popular to suggest one belongs to the "true chruch." We become uneasy and embarrassed when someone says, "You mean your's is the only true church? You think all the other churches are wrong and you're right, you're good and they're bad? You'll be the only ones saved and everyone else will be lost?" We reply, "Well, no, I don't really believe that—" What then do we believe about a "true church" on earth? Is there a special body on earth through which Christ works?

It may help to understand that God has two true churches. The term *church* is used in two very distinct ways. He has a true church we might refer to as an "invisible church," made up of everyone on this earth whom He judges as in right relationship to Himself. The members of the "invisible church" may be members of *any* denominational church, or none at all. They may be persons we would describe as heathen, having seen something of God in the order and beauty of nature, having felt the impressions of the Holy Spirit moving upon their hearts. If these impressions are followed, they will not lose their reward. There will without question be people in heaven who have never seen a Bible or heard the name of Christ. Of course, "there is none other name under heaven given among men, whereby we must be saved." Acts 4:12. No one will be saved by another than Jesus, but does this mean that they must know His name to be saved? God's true children are everywhere, and only He knows with certainty who are His, hence the term "invisible church"—not always identifiable by man, but well known to God.

But God has a "visible church" on earth as well. This is the fact with which we have some difficulty today. Some youth, and others, have wondered, "Can we really be sure which is *the* church?" While God only knows His true children everywhere, He also has always had a true visible church on earth, an identifiable, nameable movement, message, and people.

In the days of Noah there was, at the end, only one place of safety—inside the boat. Furthermore, only one message clearly identified that place. Were some of us living then, we may have considered building our own boats. If we discovered that some of them did so, I would not be surprised. Some, perhaps, made plans as a substitute for getting into the ark before the rain began to fall. Certainly many did so after. Inspiration tells us some attached themselves to the outside of the ark. Some tied their children to the backs of huge animals to be carried to the highest points of the mountains only to be swallowed up by the raging torrent. None of these substitutes worked. There is never safety in men's substitute plans of salvation. Only one message could be heeded with assurance of life—"Leave all, trust God, and prepare to enter the boat. And bring as many as you can, with the aid of the Spirit, with you into the ark of safety. Nothing else matters. When the word comes to enter, then enter, and without delay!" Only complete trust in God's movements and message through Noah could make possible such a detachment from all supposed securities of earth.

Without doubt there were some, perhaps many, who died in faith during the years of Noah's building and preaching. But ultimately there was one single door standing open "that all who would might enter, and no one was denied." The ark was not prepared simply for Noah and his family. It had room for many more. We cannot criticize God or Noah for making the boat so small that every space was filled. Furthermore, the boat could have been made larger. Or, for that matter, would not our Father, who has no pleasure in the death of the wicked, have been pleased for Noah's boat to become only the beginning of a vast fleet to ride in faith upon the stormy waters of the Flood? The ship, however large and well built, was after all only a symbol of God's care for His faithful, believing, and obedient children. A real ship, yes, yet without God's hand, helpless, in the upheavals of the Flood during which even Satan feared for his very existence. This was salvation by faith in the God who created man and who only could save him.

Today, as in pre-Flood days, and in every other age, God has used visible agencies to bring His lost children to salvation. Perhaps the open door of a church, even smaller and in some cases less inviting and more demanding than the door of the ark, will be your rescue from a lost world. Jesus described the gate and the path to life as narrow and difficult, at times appearing less pleasant than the road to destruction. Nevertheless, there is always room enough for you and me, and everyone who is willing to leave this world with all that binds him to it.

But back to the open door of the "visible church." How thankful I am that the door of a little church in Herington, Kansas, was always open when as a lad I occasionally arrived there along with my sister, my two brothers, and my mother, who was finding her way back to God after years of wandering. A small building with no children's Sabbath School, a piano in one corner which no one could play, and only an occasional visit from a district pastor. But it proved to be the gate of heaven for us.

Someone had recognized the power of an organization, a plan, a visible church with an open door. I can still hear the words sung a cappella by Mrs. McManaman, Mrs. Winters, Mrs. Berbohm, and Mrs. Corey (were there any others?) as we entered, a little late: "Welcome, welcome, ever welcome, blessed Sabbath day." As children we squirmed and thought church would never end. We giggled and were reminded on at least one occasion that we were "scaring away the angels." I can recall little enjoyment from the whole experience, except for a Sabbath meal at a member's home occasionally and a picnic once. But these church activities began a new life for us.

Mother was rebaptized. We moved to Sacramento where we attended church more regularly and later enrolled in church school. For me then came academy, college, a Christian wife, literature evangelism, ordination to the gospel ministry, mission service, academy Bible teaching, and children who hopefully will continue to follow God's path.

I thank God for His church, His schools, and His people—who are organized for service. I believe in the church visible, God's instrument for service in a dark world. I am glad that she is organized, that her doors were and are open to me and my family, and that I can have a part in keeping them open to others. Perhaps you can see now why I am somewhat of a "churchman," very defensive of the "enfeebled and defective" body God employs to proclaim a message of hope and salvation. After you understand what the church has meant to me, you can understand my concern when she and her leadership are criticized and undermined by competing "reform" groups, organizations, institutions, and publications. And I do not presume to be wise enough to identify these with certainty, nor do I believe reform, constructive criticism, the discovery of new truth, and better organization and methods to be unnecessary. Only God can judge the purposes and motives and ultimate worth of any and all of these. Perhaps they will, after all, add strength to the church. But beware of becoming too soon disillusioned with a movement, an organization, a visible church, if you please, through which God has chosen to do a special work.

"I urge those who claim to believe the truth, to walk in unity with their brethren. Do not seek to give to the world occasion to say that we are extremists, that we are disunited, that one teaches one thing, and one another. Avoid dissension. Let everyone be on guard, and be careful to be found standing in the gap to make up the breach, in place of standing at the wall seeking to make a breach. Let all be careful not to make an outcry against the only people who are fulfilling the description given of the remnant people who keep the commandments of God and have faith in Jesus, who are exalting the standard of righteousness in these last days."—*Testimonies to Ministers*, pp. 57, 58.

You will recall God's patience with Israel through Old Testament times. Seldom living up to her privileges and opportunities in proclaiming God's law and coming Messiah to the world, she nonetheless was patiently protected and nurtured by Jehovah. And when she had almost reached the point of no return, Jesus, the son of God, identified with her during the incarnation. While He faithfully called for reforms, He was careful not to disassociate Himself from her, or cause others to do so, until she had fully rejected the resurrected One who was the very foundation and purpose of her existence.

Even the apostate church of the dark ages was granted "space to repent" (Revelation 2:21), a separate, new movement being legitimate only when it became unquestionably clear that the pure gospel of salvation in Christ alone was no longer proclaimed and, in fact, not allowed.

So the Reformation churches proclaimed the gospel anew, bringing men back to a personal hope and faith in Jesus Christ, their Creator, Redeemer, King. Trusting in the services of the church, in the power of the priesthood, in the intercession of Mary and the saints, in penance and pilgrimages and indulgences could never bring peace and genuine hope. Instead there was fear and blind submission and often overwhelming guilt and despair.

The Reformation gave again the apostolic message: "Therefore being justified by faith, we have peace with God through our Lord Jesus Christ: by whom also we have access by faith into the grace wherein we stand, and rejoice in hope of the glory of God." Romans 5:1, 2. The existing church largely rejected this message and persecuted its advocates, and so a new movement was born, a new instrument to proclaim the saving gospel of Christ.

God's visible church, the church militant, in its several manifestations has always been justified in her existence only because she uniquely proclaimed the message of deliverance from sin and death. Let's review this briefly again, bringing us down through the ages to our present day.

In Noah's day there was one way, one message, one hope. All parallel or nearly right ways ended in disaster. The message of Moses again pointed man to the covenant-keeping God as the only source of deliverance from the bondage of Egypt.

At Sinai Israel discovered she was in deeper bondage than to Pharoah. She was locked in hopeless slavery to sin. This was made evident by a restatement of Jehovah's holy law and by their promise to keep it and their subsequent failure to do so. Even before it could be delivered to them engraved in stone, they failed miserably. The sacrificial services renewed and expanded at that time, of which the wilderness sanctuary, and later the temple, was the center, all had the one purpose of revealing this: A holy law, without grace, without a Saviour, could only bring death to sinful man, no matter how externally correct.

The focus of Israel should ever have been the Messiah, the Deliverer whom only their covenant-keeping God could supply. Their message was for the whole world: that the one and only Creator God would intrude into the affairs of man with the hope only He could provide. Even though they often fell and failed, God bore with them until they openly rejected their Messiah, the one name, Jesus Christ, by which man could be saved. They fully sealed their end as God's visible, salvation-proclaiming church when they rejected the message of the resurrection of Jesus and destroyed His followers.

The Christian church now arose out of Judaism to proclaim the arrival of the Messiah—His life, death, resurrection, and return—as man's only hope. As the centuries passed, the message of salvation through Christ alone became obscured, buried in a mass of tradition and ceremony. In effect man-centered and church-centered activities replaced the living Christ who only offered pardon and peace and assurance. His personal presence in the heart, available to the believer without human mediation, was largely ignored. The Reformation once again went to Scripture *alone* and brought to sinners hope in Christ *alone*. Protestantism became God's new instrument for proclaiming the everlasting gospel.

Is there need for yet another movement, for another manifestation of God's visible church? Did the Reformation churches continue to press on toward the hope of the second advent; did they continue to make the Scriptures their sole rule of faith and doctrine? Were men allowed the freedom to follow their consciences as they related personally to their Lord and Saviour? Did not the church and her dogmas in many cases once again take precedence to Scripture with the resultant persecution of dissenters? Was, indeed, the very message of justification by faith once again effectually lost sight of?

"The great doctrine of justification by faith, so clearly

taught by Luther, had been [by the time of the Wesleys and Whitefield in the mid-eighteenth century] almost wholly lost sight of; and the Romish principle of trusting to good works for salvation, had taken its place."—*The Great Controversy*, p. 253. John Wesley became "convinced that he must renounce all dependence upon his own works for salvation and must trust wholly to 'the Lamb of God, which taketh away the sin of the world.' "—Pages 255, 256. Whitefield and Wesleys again preached Christ and Him crucified.

The law and the gospel were seen to be in perfect harmony. John Wesley said, "on the one hand, the law continually makes way for, and points to, the gospel; on the other, the gospel continually leads us to a more exact fulfilling of the law. . . . 'The righteousness of the law is fulfilled in us,' through faith in Christ Jesus."—Sermon 25 (quoted in *The Great Controversy*, p. 263). Wesley saw "his strict and self-denying life, not now as the *ground*, but the *result* of faith; not the *root*, but the *fruit* of holiness. The grace of God in Christ is the foundation of the Christian's hope, and that grace will be manifested in obedience. Wesley's life was devoted to the preaching of the great truths which he had received—justification through faith in the atoning blood of Christ, and the renewing power of the Holy Spirit upon the heart bringing forth fruit in a life conformed to the example of Christ."—*The Great Controversy*, p. 256.

But even this renewal or extension of the sixteenth century Reformation did not continue. There is ever the tendency to settle down in a world of sin and lose the "first love" (Revelation 2:4), failing to allow God to finish what He has begun. In the nineteenth century the advent movement was born, proclaiming the imminent return of Christ, calling mankind to preparation for that event by confession and forsaking of sin. Salvation by faith in Christ was the message, but in the setting of the second advent. To come out of the Egyptian darkness of the church of the

Middle Ages and then cease to press on into the heavenly Canaan would indeed be a denial of the ultimate purpose of the message of righteousness by faith.

The first advent of Christ without His subsequent return to take His children home is clearly an incomplete salvation. As Donald John put it in *Insight* (December 25, 1979): "*There would not have been a First Advent if there were not going to be a second advent* [italics original]. There would be no sense to it, because both advents were designed by God to solve a problem; they are not empty exercises, not mere entertainments. . . .

"The first coming of Jesus is not an open-ended affair; it has a conclusion. . . .

". . . Because there has been a first advent, there will be a second advent. Or as Jesus Himself said, 'If I go and prepare a place for you, I will come again, and receive you unto myself; that where I am, there ye may be also' [John 14:3]."

The advent movement continues to be manifest primarily in the Seventh-day Adventist Church. Does the world need her message? Has she really anything to say that is not being loudly proclaimed by the church at large?

The airliner was already approaching the airfield in Tucson when the woman next to me said, "I don't know much about Seventh-day Adventists. What do you believe?" What was an appropriate answer for the few minutes before we would part?

I began something like this: "The *Seventh-day* in our church name refers to our observance of the Sabbath of Creation. This is not the mere keeping of a day, but a constant reminder to us that we came from somewhere, that we have a significant origin, that we don't just happen to be here, that we came from the hand of God. As you know," I continued, "most people today are not at all sure where we came from or how we got here; therefore, life has little purpose." She listened as I continued.

"That brings us to the second part of the name

Seventh-day Adventist.* *Adventist* refers to our belief in the second advent, or coming of Christ. This is our constant assurance that we are also going somewhere. We have not only an origin but a destiny. We are not lost in space." As I reminded her that most people, even Christians, have lost their hope, she said with feeling, "That's true!" She was going to Tucson to be with her daughter who had an illness which was apparently claiming her life. As we parted, she said, "Thank you, I'm glad I asked you."

We came from somewhere, and we're going somewhere? Adventists see Jesus preparing them for that future somewhere. In the most holy place of the heavenly sanctuary we see Him interceding for man in the very presence of the holy law of God, ministering His righteousness for the forgiveness of transgression of that law and bringing man once again into harmony with that law—"that the righteousness of the law might be fulfilled in us." Romans 8:4.

Adventists see themselves as heralds of the total salvation of man. They see the gospel as restoring man even now, to whatever degree possible, to health of the body, mind, and character. They see fallen mankind progressively renewed to full manhood and womanhood, not only as Adam and Eve were before the Fall, but having met the test and overcome, eventually made immortal in Christ. The saved of the earth, and all in the universe, will have so decidedly rejected sin because of what it did to Christ and His creatures, that redeemed earthlings, and all in the universe, though forever free to choose whom they will serve, *will* forever *choose* Christ and His service. Free, but immortal by choice! The "mystery of godliness"—Christ is incarnate, now forever dwelling in his earthborn creatures with a life that will not, cannot, end. What an amazing accomplishment in the prolonged great conflict

* Ellen White refers to our name as "the name the Lord has given us. It points out the truth that is to be the test of the churches."—*Selected Messages*, bk. 2, p. 384.

between Christ and Satan, the original rebel!

Yes, God has a church today to give a message for want of which the world is dying. Salvation will not come at the hands of "star trekkers" or any human attempts at legislated godliness, but freely from the hands of a loving Father who has not forgotten His children.

It need be no sign of pride to speak of a "true church" with a message of the everlasting gospel. Nor is it necessarily to one's credit to be so "humble" as to say his church is just one among many, all doing essentially the same thing. The proclamation of the three angels' messages of Revelation 14 is essential and an awesome responsibility.

To say God in every age has a true visible organization, assigned to keep alive essential truths about God and His plan of salvation, is not to suppose that no one outside that church is a true child of God or that no significant work for God is being accomplished outside that organization or body. And surely no one would suggest that within any earthly organization all is right and all are saved, however God-chosen they may believe themselves to be.

Noah and family were imperfect instruments, and doubtless they had helpers in their task who ultimately chose another way. But their work and message was ordained of God, and the final focus on the open door of the ark became a life-and-death matter.

Israel surely did not contain all who were God's or good in the world. During parts of her history she exceeded the heathen in wickedness. Nevertheless, Israel was chosen by God, who unceasingly through prophet and priest and judge and king sought to bring her to loyalty, trust, and privilege. While she often perverted God's message, the law and gospel delivered to her at Sinai were true and right and met their climax and fulfillment in the arrival of the Messiah, Jesus, the son of God, born into their very midst.

The Jewish nation ultimately rejected the gospel of Christ, but the new church grew out of the old. God apparently does not arbitrarily withdraw His support, but He finally leaves *His* chosen to what *they* have chosen. The door into the new is always first open to the remnants of the old. "Hath God cast away His people? God forbid." Romans 11:1.

The Christian church during pre-reformation days also failed in her trust to proclaim salvation in Christ alone. There was no hope of her retaining her unique, singular position.

Protestantism now undertook the task, arising out of the Christian church of the Middle Ages. Again the door was open that all who would might enter. The old gave birth to the new. Not all of Christ's true children found their way there, nor were all who found their way there Christ's true children.

When the Adventists began to proclaim the return of Christ, they had no desire to leave their churches. Had the churches of the day accepted the first angel's message, the second angel's message—"Babylon is fallen!"—would perhaps have taken on a different significance. Ideally, there would have been a united desire of all Christians to press on into the kingdom of glory, to proclaim the second advent, and God's message of preparation for it, to every nation, kindred, tongue, and people.

So today, many people within all churches, and without churches, are truly children of God. There are significant activities outside the advent movement which bring men nearer to God, to a knowledge of salvation in Christ. But the message of the second coming, with the present judgment of believers by the eternal law of God, and the message of Christ's righteousness, bringing forgiveness and also harmony with that law, must and will be proclaimed.

Faulty though the members and methods of God's church may be, there can be no substitute for her message. Eventually all men must decide for or against God's changeless law. They must decide if they will accept the

Christ who died because that law is eternal or if they will accept satanic substitutes. These subtle, deceptive alternatives are basically either salvation by man's own efforts or salvation by mere profession of the name of Christ, but without consenting to what it is His glory to do both without and within the believer. And this good news of present salvation must be proclaimed in the setting of an imminent, real bodily second advent of Jesus, a resurrection of the dead, a final destruction of sin and sinners, and a realization of immortality for believers.

As men and women become aware of this message, this movement, this people doing their unique work, what should be their response? Though not all is bad without or good within, they will count it a privilege to align themselves with this organization and join in fulfilling its awesome responsibility. God's visible church now, as always in the past, exists for a task, an assignment. Membership is not now or ever synonymous with salvation. Far from it. The following warning is to those within the church.

"Those who have drifted along, carrying no responsibility, thinking of themselves, pleasing themselves, will be placed by the Judge of all the earth with those who did evil. They receive the same condemnation. . . .

"They enjoy the services of religion. They love to hear the gospel preached, and therefore they think themselves Christians. Though they have spent their lives in caring for themselves, they will be as much surprised as was the unfaithful servant in the parable to hear the sentence, 'Take the talent from him.' [Matthew 25:13-30.] Like the Jews [of Jesus' time], they mistake the enjoyment of their blessings for the use they should make of them."

"Let none suppose that they can live a life of selfishness, and then, having served their own interests, enter into the joy of their Lord. . . . They would not be fitted for the heavenly courts. They could not appreciate the pure atmosphere of love that pervades heaven. . . . To their minds the science of heaven would be an enigma."—*Christ's*

Object Lessons, pp. 365, 364.

The church of God's appointment has never been given the task of mediating or assuring salvation to its membership, except in the sense that she proclaims Christ and puts men and women in touch with Him. The church is organized rather to accomplish a task, and any attachment to her which does not make service prominent is a perversion of the purpose of membership. "The church is to increase in activity and to enlarge her bounds. Our missionary efforts are to be expansive."—*Selected Messages*, bk. 2, p. 396.

While there is an important work to be done in the hearts of church people, we must never forget the gospel commission, "Go ye therefore." There is strength in banding together for fellowship, but no fellowship is so sweet and gives such life and strength and purpose to the believer's heart as does uniting with Christ and one another to partake with Him in His labors. This will indeed involve self-sacrifice, hardship, and deprivation at times. But it is also the highest honor, the greatest joy it is possible for God to bestow upon His disciples. *Steps to Christ*, p. 79. (See also James 1:2-4; Acts 20:24; 1 Peter 1:6-8.) "The truth is soon to triumph gloriously, and all who now choose to be laborers together with God will triumph with it."—*Testimonies*, vol. 9, p. 135.

Yes, the church is for service, appointed and protected by God to fulfill an assignment which has increasingly important significance. "He is constantly watching it with solicitude, and is strengthening it by His Holy Spirit. . . . God's eye is over His people . . . whom He is leading and instructing. . . . He has appointed that his church on earth shall stand perfectly united in the Spirit and counsel of the Lord of hosts to the end of time. Nothing in this world is so dear to God as His church."—*Selected Messages*, bk. 2, pp. 396, 397.

If God is so solicitous for the strength and unity of His church, should her members not also show the same concern? Will those who truly seek to be on God's side be drawing apart from His church, tending toward disharmony and schism? Will not all efforts at necessary reform be characterized by godly love and carefulness to stand by the church until it has been clearly shown that she can no longer be trusted with her assignment? Should we not cherish the same attitude Christ has repeatedly demonstrated toward his church, knowing she needs to be "reproved, warned, and counseled," but even this in the context of his love and "supreme regard"?—*Testimonies to Ministers*, p. 49.

R. D. Williams calls for unity of action by citing a speech of Kenya's late Jomo Kenyatta following the Mau Mau uprising.

" 'If I have done a mistake to you in the past, it is for you to forgive me. If you have done a mistake to me in the past, it is for me to forgive you. Let us now join hands and work together for the betterment of the land. I beg you to believe this will be the policy of my government. We must work together and try to trust one another.'

"Slowly but with mounting fervor the chant went up, 'Harambee! Harambee!' until everyone had joined the cry. There were no reprisals or arrests, only this outcry, 'Harambee,' which means, 'Pull together!'

" . . . What a challenge to Seventh-day Adventists . . . , to 'pull together' and finish God's work in the 80s."—

Have you become discouraged because of the delay in the coming of Christ, because of the church's seeming inability to hasten on to this objective? Surely others in times past have also felt this way, but have God's promises failed? "Cast not away therefore your confidence, which hath great recompense of reward. For ye have need of patience, that, after ye have done the will of God, ye might receive the promise. For yet a little while, and he that shall come will come, and will not tarry. Now the just shall live by faith." Hebrews 10:35-38. We have no abstract theological statement here, but a plain, practical urging of the believers in Jesus not to lose faith, courage, hope.

In 1913, two years before her death, and twenty-five years after 1888, Ellen White gave counsel to the church in General Conference session which we need today. "Cherish a spirit of hopefulness and courage. . . . Be glad in the Lord, and . . . rejoice in the knowledge of His sustaining grace. . . . Guard against becoming overwearied, careworn, depressed. Bear an uplifting testimony. Turn your eyes away from that which is dark and discouraging, and behold Jesus, our great Leader, under whose watchful supervision the cause of present truth, to which we are giving our lives and our all, is destined to triumph gloriously.

" . . . We are to move forward in faith and hope, expecting large things from God. The enemy will seek in every way to hinder the efforts that are being made to advance the truth, but in the strength of the Lord you may gain success.

"Let no discouraging words be spoken, but only such words as will tend to strengthen and sustain your fellow workers."—*Selected Messages*, bk. 2, pp. 399, 404.

Have you longed for the outpouring of the Holy Spirit upon the church—in your own life? Have you ceased to pray for this? "Fear not . . .; be glad and rejoice: for the Lord will do great things." . . . "For he hath given you the former rain moderately, and he will cause to come down for you . . . the latter rain." "I will pour out my spirit upon all flesh." Joel 2:21, 23, 28.

"The revenue of glory has been accumulating for this closing work of the third angel's message. Of the prayers that have been ascending for the fulfillment of the promise—the descent of the Holy Spirit—not one has been lost. Each prayer has been accumulating, ready to overflow and pour forth a healing flood of heavenly influence and accumulated light all over the world."—Ellen G. White, Letter 96A, 1899.

Has God forgotten His promises? Can He not fulfill

them to us? Have they lost their power and significance? Certainly not. Could we perhaps summarize the message of this book, *How to Belong When You're Already a Member*, by hearing from the prophet Joel and the apostle James?

"Therefore also now, saith the Lord, turn ye even to me with all your heart, and with fasting, and with weeping, and with mourning: and rend your heart, and not your garments, and turn unto the Lord your God: for he is gracious and merciful, slow to anger, and of great kindness." "Fear not . . .; be glad and rejoice: for the Lord will do great things." Joel 2:12, 13, 21.

"Be patient therefore, brethren, unto the coming of the Lord. Behold, the husbandman waiteth for the precious fruit of the earth, and hath long patience for it, until he receive the early and latter rain. Be ye also patient; stablish your hearts: for the coming of the Lord draweth nigh." James 5:7, 8.

Our Father, we want to be saved, and we thank You for not leaving us alone to blunder through in ignorance. We thank You for the clear messages of Scripture and for the enlightenment of the Holy Spirit sent directly to each heart, and manifest in a special way through the gift of prophecy to make things very clear. We thank you for the church, a place where we have been able to learn truth, a place where we can work for You in organized, effective, and fruitful ways. We renew our dedication to Your church, the object of Your supreme regard; we give it new regard in our own hearts today.

We long for the special outpouring of the Holy Spirit, who through Your church will cause truth to triumph; and we want to triumph with it. May none of us, like the foolish virgins, be found wanting and be lost. Forgive us for our criticisms; forgive us for not seeing Jesus and His promises but seeing instead only the defects of your people. We renew our dedication to You today. May each of us be more sure who we are, why we are here, and where we are going. May we this moment settle it in our minds that, by Your grace, we will cling to you and cooperate with You in Your efforts to save us and to save the world. May everyone reading these lines, young or old, be in your kingdom. That we may all join hands together, encourage one another, and move on into Your kingdom is our prayer in Jesus' name. Amen.